THIS IS YOUR **PASSBOOK®** FOR ...

OFFICE ASSISTANT I (KEYBOARDING)

NLC®
NATIONAL LEARNING CORPORATION®
passbooks.com

NLC®

National Learning Corporation

212 Michael Drive, Syosset, NY 11791
(516) 921-8888 • www.passbooks.com
E-mail: info@passbooks.com

PUBLISHED IN THE UNITED STATES OF AMERICA

PASSBOOK® SERIES

THE *PASSBOOK® SERIES* has been created to prepare applicants and candidates for the ultimate academic battlefield – the examination room.

At some time in our lives, each and every one of us may be required to take an examination – for validation, matriculation, admission, qualification, registration, certification, or licensure.

Based on the assumption that every applicant or candidate has met the basic formal educational standards, has taken the required number of courses, and read the necessary texts, the *PASSBOOK® SERIES* furnishes the one special preparation which may assure passing with confidence, instead of failing with insecurity. Examination questions – together with answers – are furnished as the basic vehicle for study so that the mysteries of the examination and its compounding difficulties may be eliminated or diminished by a sure method.

This book is meant to help you pass your examination provided that you qualify and are serious in your objective.

The entire field is reviewed through the huge store of content information which is succinctly presented through a provocative and challenging approach – the question-and-answer method.

A climate of success is established by furnishing the correct answers at the end of each test.

You soon learn to recognize types of questions, forms of questions, and patterns of questioning. You may even begin to anticipate expected outcomes.

You perceive that many questions are repeated or adapted so that you can gain acute insights, which may enable you to score many sure points.

You learn how to confront new questions, or types of questions, and to attack them confidently and work out the correct answers.

You note objectives and emphases, and recognize pitfalls and dangers, so that you may make positive educational adjustments.

Moreover, you are kept fully informed in relation to new concepts, methods, practices, and directions in the field.

You discover that you arre actually taking the examination all the time: you are preparing for the examination by "taking" an examination, not by reading extraneous and/or supererogatory textbooks.

In short, this PASSBOOK®, used directedly, should be an important factor in helping you to pass your test.

OFFICE ASSISTANT I (KEYBOARDING)

DUTIES:

As an Office Assistant I (Keyboarding), you would spend most of your work time performing keyboarding, data entry, chart compilation or arrangement, or tasks involving keyboarding into computerized systems. You also would perform general office support or clerical duties.

SCOPE OF THE EXAMINATION:

The multiple-choice test tests for knowledge, skills, and/or abilities in such areas as:

1. **Reading** - These questions test for the ability to read and understand short written passages. You will be asked one question about each passage. Everything you need to know to answer the question is contained in the passage. You should base your answer only on the information contained in the passage, and not on what you may know about the topic.
2. **Working with others** - These questions test for knowledge of how to interact with others in a constructive, courteous, and effective manner. Questions will involve working or interacting with a variety of individuals in a variety of circumstances.
3. **Name and number checking** - These questions test for the ability to accurately check names, words, and numbers that are almost exactly alike. Information will be presented in two or three columns. You must compare entries across the columns and mark your answers in accordance with the directions given.
4. **Operations with letters and numbers** - These questions test for the ability to perform a variety of operations using letters and numbers. You must alphabetize, arrange, compare, check, and/or count given groups of letters and/or numbers, in order to answer the questions correctly.
5. **Grammar, usage, punctuation, and spelling** - These questions test for knowledge of grammar, word usage, punctuation, and spelling in the English language. The grammar and usage questions test for the ability to recognize incorrect grammar and word usage in sentences. Questions may involve errors in agreement of subject and verb, or in the use of nouns, pronouns, verbs, adjectives, adverbs, and/or prepositions. The punctuation questions test for the ability to recognize incorrect use and placement of punctuation marks, such as commas, question marks, and quotation marks, in given sentences. The spelling questions test for the ability to identify misspelled words.

HOW TO TAKE A TEST

I. YOU MUST PASS AN EXAMINATION

A. WHAT EVERY CANDIDATE SHOULD KNOW

Examination applicants often ask us for help in preparing for the written test. What can I study in advance? What kinds of questions will be asked? How will the test be given? How will the papers be graded?

As an applicant for a civil service examination, you may be wondering about some of these things. Our purpose here is to suggest effective methods of advance study and to describe civil service examinations.

Your chances for success on this examination can be increased if you know how to prepare. Those "pre-examination jitters" can be reduced if you know what to expect. You can even experience an adventure in good citizenship if you know why civil service exams are given.

B. WHY ARE CIVIL SERVICE EXAMINATIONS GIVEN?

Civil service examinations are important to you in two ways. As a citizen, you want public jobs filled by employees who know how to do their work. As a job seeker, you want a fair chance to compete for that job on an equal footing with other candidates. The best-known means of accomplishing this two-fold goal is the competitive examination.

Exams are widely publicized throughout the nation. They may be administered for jobs in federal, state, city, municipal, town or village governments or agencies.

Any citizen may apply, with some limitations, such as the age or residence of applicants. Your experience and education may be reviewed to see whether you meet the requirements for the particular examination. When these requirements exist, they are reasonable and applied consistently to all applicants. Thus, a competitive examination may cause you some uneasiness now, but it is your privilege and safeguard.

C. HOW ARE CIVIL SERVICE EXAMS DEVELOPED?

Examinations are carefully written by trained technicians who are specialists in the field known as "psychological measurement," in consultation with recognized authorities in the field of work that the test will cover. These experts recommend the subject matter areas or skills to be tested; only those knowledges or skills important to your success on the job are included. The most reliable books and source materials available are used as references. Together, the experts and technicians judge the difficulty level of the questions.

Test technicians know how to phrase questions so that the problem is clearly stated. Their ethics do not permit "trick" or "catch" questions. Questions may have been tried out on sample groups, or subjected to statistical analysis, to determine their usefulness.

Written tests are often used in combination with performance tests, ratings of training and experience, and oral interviews. All of these measures combine to form the best-known means of finding the right person for the right job.

II. HOW TO PASS THE WRITTEN TEST

A. NATURE OF THE EXAMINATION

To prepare intelligently for civil service examinations, you should know how they differ from school examinations you have taken. In school you were assigned certain definite pages to read or subjects to cover. The examination questions were quite detailed and usually emphasized memory. Civil service exams, on the other hand, try to discover your present ability to perform the duties of a position, plus your potentiality to learn these duties. In other words, a civil service exam attempts to predict how successful you will be. Questions cover such a broad area that they cannot be as minute and detailed as school exam questions.

In the public service similar kinds of work, or positions, are grouped together in one "class." This process is known as *position-classification.* All the positions in a class are paid according to the salary range for that class. One class title covers all of these positions, and they are all tested by the same examination.

B. FOUR BASIC STEPS

1) Study the announcement

How, then, can you know what subjects to study? Our best answer is: "Learn as much as possible about the class of positions for which you've applied." The exam will test the knowledge, skills and abilities needed to do the work.

Your most valuable source of information about the position you want is the official exam announcement. This announcement lists the training and experience qualifications. Check these standards and apply only if you come reasonably close to meeting them.

The brief description of the position in the examination announcement offers some clues to the subjects which will be tested. Think about the job itself. Review the duties in your mind. Can you perform them, or are there some in which you are rusty? Fill in the blank spots in your preparation.

Many jurisdictions preview the written test in the exam announcement by including a section called "Knowledge and Abilities Required," "Scope of the Examination," or some similar heading. Here you will find out specifically what fields will be tested.

2) Review your own background

Once you learn in general what the position is all about, and what you need to know to do the work, ask yourself which subjects you already know fairly well and which need improvement. You may wonder whether to concentrate on improving your strong areas or on building some background in your fields of weakness. When the announcement has specified "some knowledge" or "considerable knowledge," or has used adjectives like "beginning principles of..." or "advanced ... methods," you can get a clue as to the number and difficulty of questions to be asked in any given field. More questions, and hence broader coverage, would be included for those subjects which are more important in the work. Now weigh your strengths and weaknesses against the job requirements and prepare accordingly.

3) Determine the level of the position

Another way to tell how intensively you should prepare is to understand the level of the job for which you are applying. Is it the entering level? In other words, is this the position in which beginners in a field of work are hired? Or is it an intermediate or advanced level? Sometimes this is indicated by such words as "Junior" or "Senior" in the class title. Other jurisdictions use Roman numerals to designate the level – Clerk I, Clerk II, for example. The word "Supervisor" sometimes appears in the title. If the level is not indicated by the title, check the description of duties. Will you be working under very close supervision, or will you have responsibility for independent decisions in this work?

4) Choose appropriate study materials

Now that you know the subjects to be examined and the relative amount of each subject to be covered, you can choose suitable study materials. For beginning level jobs, or even advanced ones, if you have a pronounced weakness in some aspect of your training, read a modern, standard textbook in that field. Be sure it is up to date and has general coverage. Such books are normally available at your library, and the librarian will be glad to help you locate one. For entry-level positions, questions of appropriate difficulty are chosen – neither highly advanced questions, nor those too simple. Such questions require careful thought but not advanced training.

If the position for which you are applying is technical or advanced, you will read more advanced, specialized material. If you are already familiar with the basic principles of your field, elementary textbooks would waste your time. Concentrate on advanced textbooks and technical periodicals. Think through the concepts and review difficult problems in your field.

These are all general sources. You can get more ideas on your own initiative, following these leads. For example, training manuals and publications of the government agency which employs workers in your field can be useful, particularly for technical and professional positions. A letter or visit to the government department involved may result in more specific study suggestions, and certainly will provide you with a more definite idea of the exact nature of the position you are seeking.

III. KINDS OF TESTS

Tests are used for purposes other than measuring knowledge and ability to perform specified duties. For some positions, it is equally important to test ability to make adjustments to new situations or to profit from training. In others, basic mental abilities not dependent on information are essential. Questions which test these things may not appear as pertinent to the duties of the position as those which test for knowledge and information. Yet they are often highly important parts of a fair examination. For very general questions, it is almost impossible to help you direct your study efforts. What we can do is to point out some of the more common of these general abilities needed in public service positions and describe some typical questions.

1) General information

Broad, general information has been found useful for predicting job success in some kinds of work. This is tested in a variety of ways, from vocabulary lists to questions about current events. Basic background in some field of work, such as sociology or economics, may be sampled in a group of questions. Often these are principles which have become familiar to most persons through exposure rather than through formal training. It is difficult to advise you how to study for these questions; being alert to the world around you is our best suggestion.

2) Verbal ability

An example of an ability needed in many positions is verbal or language ability. Verbal ability is, in brief, the ability to use and understand words. Vocabulary and grammar tests are typical measures of this ability. Reading comprehension or paragraph interpretation questions are common in many kinds of civil service tests. You are given a paragraph of written material and asked to find its central meaning.

3) Numerical ability

Number skills can be tested by the familiar arithmetic problem, by checking paired lists of numbers to see which are alike and which are different, or by interpreting charts and graphs. In the latter test, a graph may be printed in the test booklet which you are asked to use as the basis for answering questions.

4) Observation

A popular test for law-enforcement positions is the observation test. A picture is shown to you for several minutes, then taken away. Questions about the picture test your ability to observe both details and larger elements.

5) Following directions

In many positions in the public service, the employee must be able to carry out written instructions dependably and accurately. You may be given a chart with several columns, each column listing a variety of information. The questions require you to carry out directions involving the information given in the chart.

6) Skills and aptitudes

Performance tests effectively measure some manual skills and aptitudes. When the skill is one in which you are trained, such as typing or shorthand, you can practice. These tests are often very much like those given in business school or high school courses. For many of the other skills and aptitudes, however, no short-time preparation can be made. Skills and abilities natural to you or that you have developed throughout your lifetime are being tested.

Many of the general questions just described provide all the data needed to answer the questions and ask you to use your reasoning ability to find the answers. Your best preparation for these tests, as well as for tests of facts and ideas, is to be at your physical and mental best. You, no doubt, have your own methods of getting into an exam-taking mood and keeping "in shape." The next section lists some ideas on this subject.

IV. KINDS OF QUESTIONS

Only rarely is the "essay" question, which you answer in narrative form, used in civil service tests. Civil service tests are usually of the short-answer type. Full instructions for answering these questions will be given to you at the examination. But in case this is your first experience with short-answer questions and separate answer sheets, here is what you need to know:

1) Multiple-choice Questions

Most popular of the short-answer questions is the "multiple choice" or "best answer" question. It can be used, for example, to test for factual knowledge, ability to solve problems or judgment in meeting situations found at work.

A multiple-choice question is normally one of three types—

- It can begin with an incomplete statement followed by several possible endings. You are to find the one ending which *best* completes the statement, although some of the others may not be entirely wrong.
- It can also be a complete statement in the form of a question which is answered by choosing one of the statements listed.
- It can be in the form of a problem – again you select the best answer.

Here is an example of a multiple-choice question with a discussion which should give you some clues as to the method for choosing the right answer:

When an employee has a complaint about his assignment, the action which will *best* help him overcome his difficulty is to

A. discuss his difficulty with his coworkers
B. take the problem to the head of the organization
C. take the problem to the person who gave him the assignment
D. say nothing to anyone about his complaint

In answering this question, you should study each of the choices to find which is best. Consider choice "A" – Certainly an employee may discuss his complaint with fellow employees, but no change or improvement can result, and the complaint remains unresolved. Choice "B" is a poor choice since the head of the organization probably does not know what assignment you have been given, and taking your problem to him is known as "going over the head" of the supervisor. The supervisor, or person who made the assignment, is the person who can clarify it or correct any injustice. Choice "C" is, therefore, correct. To say nothing, as in choice "D," is unwise. Supervisors have and interest in knowing the problems employees are facing, and the employee is seeking a solution to his problem.

2) True/False Questions

The "true/false" or "right/wrong" form of question is sometimes used. Here a complete statement is given. Your job is to decide whether the statement is right or wrong.

SAMPLE: A roaming cell-phone call to a nearby city costs less than a non-roaming call to a distant city.

This statement is wrong, or false, since roaming calls are more expensive.

This is not a complete list of all possible question forms, although most of the others are variations of these common types. You will always get complete directions for answering questions. Be sure you understand *how* to mark your answers – ask questions until you do.

V. RECORDING YOUR ANSWERS

Computer terminals are used more and more today for many different kinds of exams.

For an examination with very few applicants, you may be told to record your answers in the test booklet itself. Separate answer sheets are much more common. If this separate answer sheet is to be scored by machine – and this is often the case – it is highly important that you mark your answers correctly in order to get credit.

An electronic scoring machine is often used in civil service offices because of the speed with which papers can be scored. Machine-scored answer sheets must be marked with a pencil, which will be given to you. This pencil has a high graphite content which responds to the electronic scoring machine. As a matter of fact, stray dots may register as answers, so do not let your pencil rest on the answer sheet while you are pondering the correct answer. Also, if your pencil lead breaks or is otherwise defective, ask for another.

Since the answer sheet will be dropped in a slot in the scoring machine, be careful not to bend the corners or get the paper crumpled.

The answer sheet normally has five vertical columns of numbers, with 30 numbers to a column. These numbers correspond to the question numbers in your test booklet. After each number, going across the page are four or five pairs of dotted lines. These short dotted lines have small letters or numbers above them. The first two pairs may also have a "T" or "F" above the letters. This indicates that the first two pairs only are to be used if the questions are of the true-false type. If the questions are multiple choice, disregard the "T" and "F" and pay attention only to the small letters or numbers.

Answer your questions in the manner of the sample that follows:

32. The largest city in the United States is
    - A. Washington, D.C.
    - B. New York City
    - C. Chicago
    - D. Detroit
    - E. San Francisco

1) Choose the answer you think is best. (New York City is the largest, so "B" is correct.)
2) Find the row of dotted lines numbered the same as the question you are answering. (Find row number 32)
3) Find the pair of dotted lines corresponding to the answer. (Find the pair of lines under the mark "B.")
4) Make a solid black mark between the dotted lines.

VI. BEFORE THE TEST

Common sense will help you find procedures to follow to get ready for an examination. Too many of us, however, overlook these sensible measures. Indeed, nervousness and fatigue have been found to be the most serious reasons why applicants fail to do their best on civil service tests. Here is a list of reminders:

- Begin your preparation early – Don't wait until the last minute to go scurrying around for books and materials or to find out what the position is all about.
- Prepare continuously – An hour a night for a week is better than an all-night cram session. This has been definitely established. What is more, a night a week for a month will return better dividends than crowding your study into a shorter period of time.
- Locate the place of the exam – You have been sent a notice telling you when and where to report for the examination. If the location is in a different town or otherwise unfamiliar to you, it would be well to inquire the best route and learn something about the building.
- Relax the night before the test – Allow your mind to rest. Do not study at all that night. Plan some mild recreation or diversion; then go to bed early and get a good night's sleep.
- Get up early enough to make a leisurely trip to the place for the test – This way unforeseen events, traffic snarls, unfamiliar buildings, etc. will not upset you.
- Dress comfortably – A written test is not a fashion show. You will be known by number and not by name, so wear something comfortable.
- Leave excess paraphernalia at home – Shopping bags and odd bundles will get in your way. You need bring only the items mentioned in the official notice you received; usually everything you need is provided. Do not bring reference books to the exam. They will only confuse those last minutes and be taken away from you when in the test room.
- Arrive somewhat ahead of time – If because of transportation schedules you must get there very early, bring a newspaper or magazine to take your mind off yourself while waiting.
- Locate the examination room – When you have found the proper room, you will be directed to the seat or part of the room where you will sit. Sometimes you are given a sheet of instructions to read while you are waiting. Do not fill out any forms until you are told to do so; just read them and be prepared.
- Relax and prepare to listen to the instructions
- If you have any physical problem that may keep you from doing your best, be sure to tell the test administrator. If you are sick or in poor health, you really cannot do your best on the exam. You can come back and take the test some other time.

VII. AT THE TEST

The day of the test is here and you have the test booklet in your hand. The temptation to get going is very strong. Caution! There is more to success than knowing the right answers. You must know how to identify your papers and understand variations in the type of short-answer question used in this particular examination. Follow these suggestions for maximum results from your efforts:

1) Cooperate with the monitor

The test administrator has a duty to create a situation in which you can be as much at ease as possible. He will give instructions, tell you when to begin, check to see that you are marking your answer sheet correctly, and so on. He is not there to guard you, although he will see that your competitors do not take unfair advantage. He wants to help you do your best.

2) Listen to all instructions

Don't jump the gun! Wait until you understand all directions. In most civil service tests you get more time than you need to answer the questions. So don't be in a hurry. Read each word of instructions until you clearly understand the meaning. Study the examples, listen to all announcements and follow directions. Ask questions if you do not understand what to do.

3) Identify your papers

Civil service exams are usually identified by number only. You will be assigned a number; you must not put your name on your test papers. Be sure to copy your number correctly. Since more than one exam may be given, copy your exact examination title.

4) Plan your time

Unless you are told that a test is a "speed" or "rate of work" test, speed itself is usually not important. Time enough to answer all the questions will be provided, but this does not mean that you have all day. An overall time limit has been set. Divide the total time (in minutes) by the number of questions to determine the approximate time you have for each question.

5) Do not linger over difficult questions

If you come across a difficult question, mark it with a paper clip (useful to have along) and come back to it when you have been through the booklet. One caution if you do this – be sure to skip a number on your answer sheet as well. Check often to be sure that you have not lost your place and that you are marking in the row numbered the same as the question you are answering.

6) Read the questions

Be sure you know what the question asks! Many capable people are unsuccessful because they failed to *read* the questions correctly.

7) Answer all questions

Unless you have been instructed that a penalty will be deducted for incorrect answers, it is better to guess than to omit a question.

8) Speed tests

It is often better NOT to guess on speed tests. It has been found that on timed tests people are tempted to spend the last few seconds before time is called in marking answers at random – without even reading them – in the hope of picking up a few extra points. To discourage this practice, the instructions may warn you that your score will be "corrected" for guessing. That is, a penalty will be applied. The incorrect answers will be deducted from the correct ones, or some other penalty formula will be used.

9) Review your answers

If you finish before time is called, go back to the questions you guessed or omitted to give them further thought. Review other answers if you have time.

10) Return your test materials

If you are ready to leave before others have finished or time is called, take ALL your materials to the monitor and leave quietly. Never take any test material with you. The monitor can discover whose papers are not complete, and taking a test booklet may be grounds for disqualification.

VIII. EXAMINATION TECHNIQUES

1) Read the general instructions carefully. These are usually printed on the first page of the exam booklet. As a rule, these instructions refer to the timing of the examination; the fact that you should not start work until the signal and must stop work at a signal, etc. If there are any *special* instructions, such as a choice of questions to be answered, make sure that you note this instruction carefully.

2) When you are ready to start work on the examination, that is as soon as the signal has been given, read the instructions to each question booklet, underline any key words or phrases, such as *least*, *best*, *outline*, *describe* and the like. In this way you will tend to answer as requested rather than discover on reviewing your paper that you *listed without describing*, that you selected the *worst* choice rather than the *best* choice, etc.

3) If the examination is of the objective or multiple-choice type – that is, each question will also give a series of possible answers: A, B, C or D, and you are called upon to select the best answer and write the letter next to that answer on your answer paper – it is advisable to start answering each question in turn. There may be anywhere from 50 to 100 such questions in the three or four hours allotted and you can see how much time would be taken if you read through all the questions before beginning to answer any. Furthermore, if you come across a question or group of questions which you know would be difficult to answer, it would undoubtedly affect your handling of all the other questions.

4) If the examination is of the essay type and contains but a few questions, it is a moot point as to whether you should read all the questions before starting to answer any one. Of course, if you are given a choice – say five out of seven and the like – then it is essential to read all the questions so you can eliminate the two that are most difficult. If, however, you are asked to answer all the questions, there may be danger in trying to answer the easiest one first because you may find that you will spend too much time on it. The best technique is to answer the first question, then proceed to the second, etc.

5) Time your answers. Before the exam begins, write down the time it started, then add the time allowed for the examination and write down the time it must be completed, then divide the time available somewhat as follows:

- If 3-1/2 hours are allowed, that would be 210 minutes. If you have 80 objective-type questions, that would be an average of 2-1/2 minutes per question. Allow yourself no more than 2 minutes per question, or a total of 160 minutes, which will permit about 50 minutes to review.
- If for the time allotment of 210 minutes there are 7 essay questions to answer, that would average about 30 minutes a question. Give yourself only 25 minutes per question so that you have about 35 minutes to review.

6) The most important instruction is to *read each question* and make sure you know what is wanted. The second most important instruction is to *time yourself properly* so that you answer every question. The third most important instruction is to *answer every question.* Guess if you have to but include something for each question. Remember that you will receive no credit for a blank and will probably receive some credit if you write something in answer to an essay question. If you guess a letter – say "B" for a multiple-choice question – you may have guessed right. If you leave a blank as an answer to a multiple-choice question, the examiners may respect your feelings but it will not add a point to your score. Some exams may penalize you for wrong answers, so in such cases *only,* you may not want to guess unless you have some basis for your answer.

7) Suggestions
   a. Objective-type questions
      1. Examine the question booklet for proper sequence of pages and questions
      2. Read all instructions carefully
      3. Skip any question which seems too difficult; return to it after all other questions have been answered
      4. Apportion your time properly; do not spend too much time on any single question or group of questions
      5. Note and underline key words – *all, most, fewest, least, best, worst, same, opposite,* etc.
      6. Pay particular attention to negatives
      7. Note unusual option, e.g., unduly long, short, complex, different or similar in content to the body of the question
      8. Observe the use of "hedging" words – *probably, may, most likely,* etc.
      9. Make sure that your answer is put next to the same number as the question
      10. Do not second-guess unless you have good reason to believe the second answer is definitely more correct
      11. Cross out original answer if you decide another answer is more accurate; do not erase until you are ready to hand your paper in
      12. Answer all questions; guess unless instructed otherwise
      13. Leave time for review

   b. Essay questions
      1. Read each question carefully
      2. Determine exactly what is wanted. Underline key words or phrases.
      3. Decide on outline or paragraph answer

4. Include many different points and elements unless asked to develop any one or two points or elements
5. Show impartiality by giving pros and cons unless directed to select one side only
6. Make and write down any assumptions you find necessary to answer the questions
7. Watch your English, grammar, punctuation and choice of words
8. Time your answers; don't crowd material

8) Answering the essay question

Most essay questions can be answered by framing the specific response around several key words or ideas. Here are a few such key words or ideas:

M's: manpower, materials, methods, money, management
P's: purpose, program, policy, plan, procedure, practice, problems, pitfalls, personnel, public relations

a. Six basic steps in handling problems:
   1. Preliminary plan and background development
   2. Collect information, data and facts
   3. Analyze and interpret information, data and facts
   4. Analyze and develop solutions as well as make recommendations
   5. Prepare report and sell recommendations
   6. Install recommendations and follow up effectiveness

b. Pitfalls to avoid
   1. *Taking things for granted* – A statement of the situation does not necessarily imply that each of the elements is necessarily true; for example, a complaint may be invalid and biased so that all that can be taken for granted is that a complaint has been registered
   2. *Considering only one side of a situation* – Wherever possible, indicate several alternatives and then point out the reasons you selected the best one
   3. *Failing to indicate follow up* – Whenever your answer indicates action on your part, make certain that you will take proper follow-up action to see how successful your recommendations, procedures or actions turn out to be
   4. *Taking too long in answering any single question* – Remember to time your answers properly

IX. AFTER THE TEST

Scoring procedures differ in detail among civil service jurisdictions although the general principles are the same. Whether the papers are hand-scored or graded by machine we have described, they are nearly always graded by number. That is, the person who marks the paper knows only the number – never the name – of the applicant. Not until all the papers have been graded will they be matched with names. If other tests, such as training and experience or oral interview ratings have been given, scores will be combined. Different parts of the examination usually have different weights. For example, the written test might count 60 percent of the final grade, and a rating of training and experience 40 percent. In many jurisdictions, veterans will have a certain number of points added to their grades.

After the final grade has been determined, the names are placed in grade order and an eligible list is established. There are various methods for resolving ties between those who get the same final grade – probably the most common is to place first the name of the person whose application was received first. Job offers are made from the eligible list in the order the names appear on it. You will be notified of your grade and your rank as soon as all these computations have been made. This will be done as rapidly as possible.

People who are found to meet the requirements in the announcement are called "eligibles." Their names are put on a list of eligible candidates. An eligible's chances of getting a job depend on how high he stands on this list and how fast agencies are filling jobs from the list.

When a job is to be filled from a list of eligibles, the agency asks for the names of people on the list of eligibles for that job. When the civil service commission receives this request, it sends to the agency the names of the three people highest on this list. Or, if the job to be filled has specialized requirements, the office sends the agency the names of the top three persons who meet these requirements from the general list.

The appointing officer makes a choice from among the three people whose names were sent to him. If the selected person accepts the appointment, the names of the others are put back on the list to be considered for future openings.

That is the rule in hiring from all kinds of eligible lists, whether they are for typist, carpenter, chemist, or something else. For every vacancy, the appointing officer has his choice of any one of the top three eligibles on the list. This explains why the person whose name is on top of the list sometimes does not get an appointment when some of the persons lower on the list do. If the appointing officer chooses the second or third eligible, the No. 1 eligible does not get a job at once, but stays on the list until he is appointed or the list is terminated.

X. HOW TO PASS THE INTERVIEW TEST

The examination for which you applied requires an oral interview test. You have already taken the written test and you are now being called for the interview test – the final part of the formal examination.

You may think that it is not possible to prepare for an interview test and that there are no procedures to follow during an interview. Our purpose is to point out some things you can do in advance that will help you and some good rules to follow and pitfalls to avoid while you are being interviewed.

What is an interview supposed to test?

The written examination is designed to test the technical knowledge and competence of the candidate; the oral is designed to evaluate intangible qualities, not readily measured otherwise, and to establish a list showing the relative fitness of each candidate – as measured against his competitors – for the position sought. Scoring is not on the basis of "right" and "wrong," but on a sliding scale of values ranging from "not passable" to "outstanding." As a matter of fact, it is possible to achieve a relatively low score without a single "incorrect" answer because of evident weakness in the qualities being measured.

Occasionally, an examination may consist entirely of an oral test – either an individual or a group oral. In such cases, information is sought concerning the technical knowledges and abilities of the candidate, since there has been no written examination for this purpose. More commonly, however, an oral test is used to supplement a written examination.

Who conducts interviews?

The composition of oral boards varies among different jurisdictions. In nearly all, a representative of the personnel department serves as chairman. One of the members of the board may be a representative of the department in which the candidate would work. In some cases, "outside experts" are used, and, frequently, a businessman or some other representative of the general public is asked to serve. Labor and management or other special groups may be represented. The aim is to secure the services of experts in the appropriate field.

However the board is composed, it is a good idea (and not at all improper or unethical) to ascertain in advance of the interview who the members are and what groups they represent. When you are introduced to them, you will have some idea of their backgrounds and interests, and at least you will not stutter and stammer over their names.

What should be done before the interview?

While knowledge about the board members is useful and takes some of the surprise element out of the interview, there is other preparation which is more substantive. It *is* possible to prepare for an oral interview – in several ways:

1) Keep a copy of your application and review it carefully before the interview

This may be the only document before the oral board, and the starting point of the interview. Know what education and experience you have listed there, and the sequence and dates of all of it. Sometimes the board will ask you to review the highlights of your experience for them; you should not have to hem and haw doing it.

2) Study the class specification and the examination announcement

Usually, the oral board has one or both of these to guide them. The qualities, characteristics or knowledges required by the position sought are stated in these documents. They offer valuable clues as to the nature of the oral interview. For example, if the job involves supervisory responsibilities, the announcement will usually indicate that knowledge of modern supervisory methods and the qualifications of the candidate as a supervisor will be tested. If so, you can expect such questions, frequently in the form of a hypothetical situation which you are expected to solve. NEVER go into an oral without knowledge of the duties and responsibilities of the job you seek.

3) Think through each qualification required

Try to visualize the kind of questions you would ask if you were a board member. How well could you answer them? Try especially to appraise your own knowledge and background in each area, *measured against the job sought*, and identify any areas in which you are weak. Be critical and realistic – do not flatter yourself.

4) Do some general reading in areas in which you feel you may be weak

For example, if the job involves supervision and your past experience has NOT, some general reading in supervisory methods and practices, particularly in the field of human relations, might be useful. Do NOT study agency procedures or detailed manuals. The oral board will be testing your understanding and capacity, not your memory.

5) Get a good night's sleep and watch your general health and mental attitude

You will want a clear head at the interview. Take care of a cold or any other minor ailment, and of course, no hangovers.

What should be done on the day of the interview?

Now comes the day of the interview itself. Give yourself plenty of time to get there. Plan to arrive somewhat ahead of the scheduled time, particularly if your appointment is in the fore part of the day. If a previous candidate fails to appear, the board might be ready for you a bit early. By early afternoon an oral board is almost invariably behind schedule if there are many candidates, and you may have to wait. Take along a book or magazine to read, or your application to review, but leave any extraneous material in the waiting room when you go in for your interview. In any event, relax and compose yourself.

The matter of dress is important. The board is forming impressions about you – from your experience, your manners, your attitude, and your appearance. Give your personal appearance careful attention. Dress your best, but not your flashiest. Choose conservative, appropriate clothing, and be sure it is immaculate. This is a business interview, and your appearance should indicate that you regard it as such. Besides, being well groomed and properly dressed will help boost your confidence.

Sooner or later, someone will call your name and escort you into the interview room. *This is it.* From here on you are on your own. It is too late for any more preparation. But remember, you asked for this opportunity to prove your fitness, and you are here because your request was granted.

What happens when you go in?

The usual sequence of events will be as follows: The clerk (who is often the board stenographer) will introduce you to the chairman of the oral board, who will introduce you to the other members of the board. Acknowledge the introductions before you sit down. Do not be surprised if you find a microphone facing you or a stenotypist sitting by. Oral interviews are usually recorded in the event of an appeal or other review.

Usually the chairman of the board will open the interview by reviewing the highlights of your education and work experience from your application – primarily for the benefit of the other members of the board, as well as to get the material into the record. Do not interrupt or comment unless there is an error or significant misinterpretation; if that is the case, do not hesitate. But do not quibble about insignificant matters. Also, he will usually ask you some question about your education, experience or your present job – partly to get you to start talking and to establish the interviewing "rapport." He may start the actual questioning, or turn it over to one of the other members. Frequently, each member undertakes the questioning on a particular area, one in which he is perhaps most competent, so you can expect each member to participate in the examination. Because time is limited, you may also expect some rather abrupt switches in the direction the questioning takes, so do not be upset by it. Normally, a board member will not pursue a single line of questioning unless he discovers a particular strength or weakness.

After each member has participated, the chairman will usually ask whether any member has any further questions, then will ask you if you have anything you wish to add. Unless you are expecting this question, it may floor you. Worse, it may start you off on an extended, extemporaneous speech. The board is not usually seeking more information. The question is principally to offer you a last opportunity to present further qualifications or to indicate that you have nothing to add. So, if you feel that a significant qualification or characteristic has been overlooked, it is proper to point it out in a sentence or so. Do not compliment the board on the thoroughness of their examination – they have been sketchy, and you know it. If you wish, merely say, "No thank you, I have nothing further to add." This is a point where you can "talk yourself out" of a good impression or fail to present an important bit of information. Remember, *you close the interview yourself.*

The chairman will then say, "That is all, Mr. ______, thank you." Do not be startled; the interview is over, and quicker than you think. Thank him, gather your belongings and take your leave. Save your sigh of relief for the other side of the door.

How to put your best foot forward

Throughout this entire process, you may feel that the board individually and collectively is trying to pierce your defenses, seek out your hidden weaknesses and embarrass and confuse you. Actually, this is not true. They are obliged to make an appraisal of your qualifications for the job you are seeking, and they want to see you in your best light. Remember, they must interview all candidates and a non-cooperative candidate may become a failure in spite of their best efforts to bring out his qualifications. Here are 15 suggestions that will help you:

1) Be natural – Keep your attitude confident, not cocky

If you are not confident that you can do the job, do not expect the board to be. Do not apologize for your weaknesses, try to bring out your strong points. The board is interested in a positive, not negative, presentation. Cockiness will antagonize any board member and make him wonder if you are covering up a weakness by a false show of strength.

2) Get comfortable, but don't lounge or sprawl

Sit erectly but not stiffly. A careless posture may lead the board to conclude that you are careless in other things, or at least that you are not impressed by the importance of the occasion. Either conclusion is natural, even if incorrect. Do not fuss with your clothing, a pencil or an ashtray. Your hands may occasionally be useful to emphasize a point; do not let them become a point of distraction.

3) Do not wisecrack or make small talk

This is a serious situation, and your attitude should show that you consider it as such. Further, the time of the board is limited – they do not want to waste it, and neither should you.

4) Do not exaggerate your experience or abilities

In the first place, from information in the application or other interviews and sources, the board may know more about you than you think. Secondly, you probably will not get away with it. An experienced board is rather adept at spotting such a situation, so do not take the chance.

5) If you know a board member, do not make a point of it, yet do not hide it

Certainly you are not fooling him, and probably not the other members of the board. Do not try to take advantage of your acquaintanceship – it will probably do you little good.

6) Do not dominate the interview

Let the board do that. They will give you the clues – do not assume that you have to do all the talking. Realize that the board has a number of questions to ask you, and do not try to take up all the interview time by showing off your extensive knowledge of the answer to the first one.

7) Be attentive

You only have 20 minutes or so, and you should keep your attention at its sharpest throughout. When a member is addressing a problem or question to you, give him your undivided attention. Address your reply principally to him, but do not exclude the other board members.

8) Do not interrupt

A board member may be stating a problem for you to analyze. He will ask you a question when the time comes. Let him state the problem, and wait for the question.

9) Make sure you understand the question

Do not try to answer until you are sure what the question is. If it is not clear, restate it in your own words or ask the board member to clarify it for you. However, do not haggle about minor elements.

10) Reply promptly but not hastily

A common entry on oral board rating sheets is "candidate responded readily," or "candidate hesitated in replies." Respond as promptly and quickly as you can, but do not jump to a hasty, ill-considered answer.

11) Do not be peremptory in your answers

A brief answer is proper – but do not fire your answer back. That is a losing game from your point of view. The board member can probably ask questions much faster than you can answer them.

12) Do not try to create the answer you think the board member wants

He is interested in what kind of mind you have and how it works – not in playing games. Furthermore, he can usually spot this practice and will actually grade you down on it.

13) Do not switch sides in your reply merely to agree with a board member

Frequently, a member will take a contrary position merely to draw you out and to see if you are willing and able to defend your point of view. Do not start a debate, yet do not surrender a good position. If a position is worth taking, it is worth defending.

14) Do not be afraid to admit an error in judgment if you are shown to be wrong

The board knows that you are forced to reply without any opportunity for careful consideration. Your answer may be demonstrably wrong. If so, admit it and get on with the interview.

15) Do not dwell at length on your present job

The opening question may relate to your present assignment. Answer the question but do not go into an extended discussion. You are being examined for a *new* job, not your present one. As a matter of fact, try to phrase ALL your answers in terms of the job for which you are being examined.

Basis of Rating

Probably you will forget most of these "do's" and "don'ts" when you walk into the oral interview room. Even remembering them all will not ensure you a passing grade. Perhaps you did not have the qualifications in the first place. But remembering them will help you to put your best foot forward, without treading on the toes of the board members.

Rumor and popular opinion to the contrary notwithstanding, an oral board wants you to make the best appearance possible. They know you are under pressure – but they also want to see how you respond to it as a guide to what your reaction would be under the pressures of the job you seek. They will be influenced by the degree of poise you display, the personal traits you show and the manner in which you respond.

ABOUT THIS BOOK

This book contains tests divided into Examination Sections. Go through each test, answering every question in the margin. At the end of each test look at the answer key and check your answers. On the ones you got wrong, look at the right answer choice and learn. Do not fill in the answers first. Do not memorize the questions and answers, but understand the answer and principles involved. On your test, the questions will likely be different from the samples. Questions are changed and new ones added. If you understand these past questions you should have success with any changes that arise. Tests may consist of several types of questions. We have additional books on each subject should more study be advisable or necessary for you. Finally, the more you study, the better prepared you will be. This book is intended to be the last thing you study before you walk into the examination room. Prior study of relevant texts is also recommended. NLC publishes some of these in our Fundamental Series. Knowledge and good sense are important factors in passing your exam. Good luck also helps. So now study this Passbook, absorb the material contained within and take that knowledge into the examination. Then do your best to pass that exam.

EXAMINATION SECTION

EXAMINATION SECTION

TEST 1

DIRECTIONS: Each question or incomplete statement is followed by several suggested answers or completions. Select the one that BEST answers the question or completes the statement. *PRINT THE LETTER OF THE CORRECT ANSWER IN THE SPACE AT THE RIGHT.*

1. The one of the following that is MOST advisable to do before transcribing your dictation notes is to — 1.______
   A. check the syllabification of long words for typing purposes
   B. edit your notes
   C. number the pages of dictation
   D. sort them by the kind of typing format required

2. As a secretary, the one of the following which is LEAST important in writing a letter under your own signature is — 2.______
   A. the accuracy of the information
   B. the appropriateness of the language
   C. the reason for the letter
   D. your supervisor's approval of the final copy

3. In a typed letter, the reference line is used — 3.______
   A. for identification purposes on typed pages of more than one page
   B. to indicate under what heading the copy of the letter should be filed
   C. to indicate who dictated the letter and who typed it
   D. to make the subject of the letter prominent by typing it a single space below the salutation

Questions 4-5:

DIRECTIONS: For questions 4 and 5, choose the letter of the sentence that BEST and MOST clearly expresses its meaning.

4. — 4.______
   A. It has always been the practice of this office to effectuate recruitment of prospective employees from other departments.
   B. This office has always made a practice of recruiting prospective employees from other departments.
   C. Recruitment of prospective employees from other departments has always been a practice which has been implemented by this office.
   D. Implementation of the policy of recruitment of prospective employees from other departments has always been a practice of this office.

5. A. These employees are assigned to the level of work evidenced by their efforts and skills during the training period. 5.______
   B. The level of work to which these employees is assigned is decided upon on the basis of the efforts and skills evidenced by them during the period in which they were trained.
   C. Assignment of these employees is made on the basis of the level of work their efforts and skills during the training period has evidenced.
   D. These employees are assigned to a level of work their efforts and skills during the training period have evidenced.

6. An office assistant was asked to mail a duplicated report of 100 pages to a professor in an out-of-town university. The professor sending the report dictated a short letter that he wanted to mail with the report. 6.______
   Of the following, the MOST inexpensive proper means of sending these two items would be to send the report
   A. and the letter first class
   B. by parcel post and the letter separately by air mail
   C. and the letter by parcel post
   D. by parcel post and attach to the package an envelope with first-class postage in which is enclosed the letter

7. Plans are underway to determine the productivity of the typists who work in a central office. Of the procedures listed, the one generally considered the MOST accurate for finding out the typists' output is to 7.______
   A. keep a record of how much typing is done over specified periods of time
   B. ask each typist how fast she types when she is doing a great deal of word processing
   C. give each typist a timed test during a specified period
   D. ask the supervisor to estimate the typing speed of each subordinate

8. Assume that an executive regularly receives the four types of mail listed below. 8.______
   As a general rule, the executive's secretary should arrange the mail from top to bottom so that the top items are
   A. advertisements
   B. airmail letters
   C. business letters
   D. unopened personal letters

9. An office assistant in transcribing reports and letters from dictation should MOST generally assume that 9.______
   A. the transcript should be exactly what was dictated so there is little need to check any details
   B. the dictated material is merely an idea of what the dictator wanted to say so changes should be made to improve any part of the dictation
   C. there may be some slight changes, but essentially the transcription is to be a faithful copy of what was dictated
   D. the transcript is merely a very rough draft and should be typed quickly so that the dictator can review it and make changes preliminary to having the final copy typed

10. The one of the following which generally is the CHIEF disadvantage of using office machines in place of human workers in office work is that the machines are 10.______
   A. slower
   B. less accurate
   C. more costly
   D. less flexible

11. An office assistant in a New York City college is asked to place a call to a prospective visiting professor in Los Angeles. It is 1 p.m. in New York (EST). The time in Los Angeles is 11.______
   A. 9 a.m.
   B. 10 a.m.
   C. 4 p.m.
   D. 5 p.m.

12. An office assistant is instructed to send a copy of a report to a professor located in a building across campus. The fastest and most efficient way for this report to reach the professor is by 12.______
   A. sending a messenger to hand-deliver it to the professor's office
   B. sending it via fax to the main office of the professor's department
   C. e-mailing it to the professor
   D. dictating the contents of the report to the professor over the phone

13. An office assistant is in the process of typing the forms for recommendation for promotion for a member of the faculty who is away for a week. She notes that two books of which he is the author are listed without dates. 13.______
Of the following, the procedure she should BEST follow at this point generally is to
   A. postpone doing the job until the professor returns to campus the following week
   B. type the material omitting the books
   C. check the professor's office for copies of the books and obtain the correct data
   D. call the professor's wife and ask her when the books were published

14. An office has introduced work standards for all of the employees. 14.______
Of the following, it is MOST likely that use of such standards would tend to
    A. make it more difficult to determine numbers of employees needed
    B. lead to a substantial drop in morale among all of the employees
    C. reduce the possibility of planning to meet emergencies
    D. reduce uncertainty about the costs of doing tasks

15. Of the following clerical errors, the one which probably is LEAST important is 15.______
    A. adding 543 instead of 548 to a bookkeeping account
    B. putting the wrong code on a data processing card
    C. recording a transaction on the record of Henry Smith instead of on the record of Harry Smith
    D. writing John Murpfy instead of John Murphy when addressing an envelope

16. Of the following errors, the one which probably is MOST important is 16.______
    A. writing "they're" instead of "their" in an office memo
    B. misplacing a decimal point on a sales invoice
    C. forgetting to write the date on a note for a supervisor
    D. sending an e-mail to a misspelled e-mail address

17. The chairman of an academic department tells an office assistant that a meeting of the faculty is to be held four weeks from the current date. 17.______
Of the following responsibilities, the office assistant is MOST frequently held responsible for
    A. planning the agenda of the meeting
    B. presiding over the conduct of the meeting
    C. reserving the meeting room and notifying the members
    D. initiating all formal resolutions

18. Of the following, a centralized filing system is LEAST suitable for filing 18.______
    A. material which is confidential in nature
    B. routine correspondence
    C. periodic reports of the divisions of the department
    D. material used by several divisions of the department

19. A misplaced record is a lost record. 19.______
Of the following, the MOST valid implication of this statement in regard to office work is that
    A. all records in an office should be filed in strict alphabetical order
    B. accuracy in filing is essential
    C. only one method of filing should be used throughout the office
    D. files should be locked when not in use

20. When typing names or titles on a roll of folder labels, the one of the following which is MOST important to do is to type the caption 20.______
    A. as it appears on the papers to be placed in the folder
    B. in capital letters
    C. in exact indexing or filing order
    D. so that it appears near the bottom of the folder tab when the label is attached

21. A professor at a Boston university asks an office assistant to place a call to a fellow professor in San Francisco. The MOST appropriate local time for the assistant to place the call to the professor in California, given the time difference, would be 21.______
    A. 8:30 a.m. B. 10:00 a.m. C. 11:30 a.m. D. 1:30 p.m.

22. When typing the rough draft of a report, the computer application you would use is 22.______
    A. Excel
    B. Word
    C. PowerPoint
    D. Internet Explorer

23. Which of the following is the BEST and most appropriate way to proofread and edit a report before submitting it to a supervisor for review? 23.______
    A. Scan the report with the program's spell check feature
    B. Proof the report yourself, then ask another office assistant to read the report over as well until it is finished
    C. Give the report to another office assistant who is more skilled at proofreading
    D. Use the spell checker, then scan the report yourself as many times as needed in order to pick up any additional errors

24. The one of the following situations in which it would be MOST justifiable for an office to use standard or form paragraphs in its business letters is when 24.______
    A. a large number of similar letters is to be sent
    B. the letters are to be uniform in length and appearance
    C. it is desired to reduce typing errors in correspondence
    D. the office is to carry on a lengthy correspondence with an individual

25. Of the following, the MOST important factor in determining whether or not an office filing system is effective is that the 25.______
    A. information in the files is legible
    B. records in the files are used frequently
    C. information in the files is accurate
    D. records in the files can be located readily

KEY (CORRECT ANSWERS)

1. B	11. B	21. D
2. D	12. C	22. B
3. C	13. C	23. D
4. B	14. D	24. A
5. A	15. D	25. D
6. D	16. B	
7. A	17. C	
8. D	18. A	
9. C	19. B	
10. D	20. C	

TEST 2

DIRECTIONS: Each question or incomplete statement is followed by several suggested answers or completions. Select the one that BEST answers the question or completes the statement. *PRINT THE LETTER OF THE CORRECT ANSWER IN THE SPACE AT THE RIGHT.*

1. For the office assistant whose duties include frequent recording and transcription of minutes of formal meetings, the one of the following reference works generally considered to be MOST useful is 1.______
   A. *Robert's Rules of Order*
   B. *Bartlett's Familiar Quotations*
   C. *World Almanac and Book of Facts*
   D. *Conway's Reference*

2. Of the following statements about the numeric system of filing, the one which is CORRECT is that it 2.______
   A. is the least accurate of all methods of filing
   B. eliminates the need for cross-referencing
   C. allows for very limited expansion
   D. requires a separate index

3. When more than one name or subject is involved in a piece of correspondence to be filed, the office assistant should GENERALLY 3.______
   A. prepare a cross-reference sheet
   B. establish a geographical filing system
   C. prepare out-guides
   D. establish a separate index card file for noting such correspondence

4. A tickler file is MOST generally used for 4.______
   A. identification of material contained in a numeric file
   B. maintenance of a current listing of telephone numbers
   C. follow-up of matters requiring future attention
   D. control of records borrowed or otherwise removed from the files

5. In filing, the name Ms. *Ann Catalana-Moss* should GENERALLY be indexed as 5.______
   A. Moss, Catalana, Ann (Ms.)
   B. Catalana-Moss, Ann (Ms.)
   C. Ann Catalana-Moss (Ms.)
   D. Moss-Catalana, Ann (Ms.)

6. An office assistant has a set of four cards, each of which contains one of the following names. 6.______
In alphabetic filing, the FIRST of the cards to be filed is
   A. Ms. Alma John
   B. Mrs. John (Patricia) Edwards
   C. John-Edward School Supplies, Inc.
   D. John H. Edwards

7. Generally, of the following, the name to be filed FIRST in an alphabetical filing system is 7.______
   A. Diane Maestro
   B. Diana McElroy
   C. James Mackell
   D. James McKell

8. After checking several times, you are unable to locate a student record in its proper file drawer. The file drawer in question is used constantly by many members of the staff. 8.______
In this situation, the NEXT step you should take in locating the missing record is to
   A. ask another worker to look through the file drawer
   B. determine if there is another copy of the record filed in a different place
   C. find out if the record has been removed by another staff member
   D. wait a day or two and see if the record turns up

9. It is MOST important that an enclosure which is to be mailed with a letter should be put in an envelope so that 9.______
   A. any printing on the enclosure will not be visible through the address side of the envelope
   B. it is obvious that there is an enclosure inside the envelope
   C. the enclosure takes up less space than the letter
   D. the person who opens the envelope will pull out both the letter and the enclosure

10. Suppose that one of the student aides with whom you work suggests a change in the filing procedure. He is sure the change will result in increased rates of filing among the other employees. 10.______
The one of the following which you should do FIRST is to
   A. ask him to demonstrate his method in order to determine if he files more quickly than the other employees
   B. ask your supervisor if you may make a change in the filing procedure
   C. ignore the aide's suggestion since he is not a filing expert
   D. tell him to show his method to the other employees and to encourage them to use it

11. It is generally advisable to leave at least six inches of working space in a file drawer. This procedure is MOST useful in 11.______
    A. decreasing the number of filing errors
    B. facilitating the sorting of documents and folders
    C. maintaining a regular program of removing inactive records
    D. preventing folders and papers from being torn

12. Assume that a dictator is briefly interrupted because of a telephone call or other similar matter (no more than three minutes). 12.______
    Of the following tasks, the person taking the dictation should NORMALLY use the time to
    A. re-read notes already recorded
    B. tidy the dictator's desk
    C. check the accuracy of the dictator's desk files
    D. return to her own desk to type the dictated material

13. When typing a preliminary draft of a report, the one of the following which you should generally NOT do is 13.______
    A. erase typing errors and deletions rather than cross them out
    B. leave plenty of room at the top, bottom and sides of each page
    C. make only the number of copies that you are asked to make
    D. type double or triple space

14. The BEST way for a receptionist to deal with a situation in which she must leave her desk for a long time is to 14.______
    A. ask someone to take her place while she is away
    B. leave a note or sign on her desk which indicates the time she will return
    C. take a chance that no one will arrive while she is gone and leave her desk unattended
    D. tell a coworker to ask any visitors that arrive to wait until she returns

15. Suppose that two individuals come up to your desk at the same time. One of them asks you for the location of the nearest public phone. After you answer the question, you turn to the second person who asks you the same question. 15.______
    The one of the following actions that would be BEST for you to take in this situation is to
    A. ignore the second person since he obviously overheard your first answer
    B. point out that you just answered the same question and quickly repeat the information
    C. politely repeat the information to the second individual
    D. tell the second person to follow the first to the public telephone

16. Which of the following names should be filed FIRST in an alphabetical filing system? 16.______
    A. Anthony Aarvedsen
    B. William Aaron
    C. Denise Aron
    D. A.J. Arrington

17. New material added to a file folder should USUALLY be inserted 17.______
    A. in the order of importance (the most important in front)
    B. in the order of importance (the most important in back)
    C. chronologically (most recent in front)
    D. chronologically (most recent in back)

18. An individual is looking for a name in the White Pages of a telephone directory. 18.______
    Which of the following BEST describes the system of filing found there?
    A. alphabetic
    B. sequential
    C. locator
    D. index

19. The MAIN purpose of a tickler file is to 19.______
    A. help prevent overlooking matters that require future attention
    B. check on adequacy of past performance
    C. pinpoint responsibility for recurring daily tasks
    D. reduce the volume of material kept in general files

20. Which of the following BEST describes the process of *reconciling* a bank statement? 20.______
    A. Analyzing the nature of the expenditures made by the office during the preceding month
    B. Comparing the statement of the bank with the banking records maintained in the office
    C. Determining the liquidity position by reading the bank statement carefully
    D. Checking the service charges noted on the bank statement

21. From the viewpoint of preserving agency or institutional funds, the LEAST acceptable method for making a payment is a check made out to 21.______
    A. cash
    B. a company
    C. an individual
    D. a partnership

22. Listed below are four of the steps in the process of preparing correspondence for filing. 22.______
    If they were to be put in logical sequence, the SECOND step would be
    A. preparing cross-reference sheets or cards
    B. coding the correspondence using a classification system
    C. sorting the correspondence in the order to be filed
    D. checking for follow-up action required and preparing a follow-up slip

23. The process of *justifying* typed copy involves laying out the copy so that 23.______
    A. each paragraph appears to be approximately the same size
    B. no long words are broken up at the end of a line
    C. the right and left hand margins are even
    D. there is enough room to enter proofreading marks at the end of each line

24. The MOST important reason for a person in charge of a petty cash fund to obtain receipts for payments is that this practice would tend to 24.______
    A. decrease robberies by delivery personnel
    B. eliminate the need to keep a record of petty cash expenditures
    C. prove that the fund has been used properly
    D. provide a record of the need for cash in the daily operations of the office

25. You should GENERALLY replenish a petty cash fund 25.______
    A. at regularly established intervals
    B. each time you withdraw a sum
    C. when the amount of cash gets below a certain specified amount
    D. when the fund is completely empty

KEY (CORRECT ANSWERS)

1. A	11. D	21. A
2. D	12. A	22. A
3. A	13. A	23. C
4. C	14. A	24. C
5. B	15. C	25. C
6. D	16. B	
7. C	17. C	
8. C	18. A	
9. D	19. A	
10. A	20. B	

EXAMINATION SECTION
TEST 1

DIRECTIONS: Each question or incomplete statement is followed by several suggested answers or completions. Select the one that BEST answers the question or completes the statement. *PRINT THE LETTER OF THE CORRECT ANSWER IN THE SPACE AT THE RIGHT.*

1. If you open a personal letter by mistake, the one of the following actions which it would generally be BEST for you to take is to 1.____

   A. ignore your error, attach the envelope to the letter, and distribute in the usual manner
   B. personally give the addressee the letter without any explanation
   C. place the letter inside the envelope, indicate under your initials that it was opened in error, and give to the addressee
   D. reseal the envelope or place the contents in another envelope and pass on to addressee

2. If you receive a telephone call regarding a matter which your office does not handle, you should FIRST 2.____

   A. give the caller the telephone number of the proper office so that he can dial again
   B. offer to transfer the caller to the proper office
   C. suggest that the caller re-dial since he probably dialed incorrectly
   D. tell the caller he has reached the wrong office and then hang up

3. When you answer the telephone, the MOST important reason for identifying yourself and your organization is to 3.____

   A. give the caller time to collect his or her thoughts
   B. impress the caller with your courtesy
   C. inform the caller that he or she has reached the right number
   D. set a business-like tone at the beginning of the conversation

4. The one of the following cases in which you would NOT place a special notation in the left margin of a letter that you have typed is when 4.____

   A. one of the copies is intended for someone other than the addressee of the letter
   B. you enclose a flyer with the letter
   C. you sign your superior's name to the letter, at his or her request
   D. the letter refers to something being sent under separate cover

5. Suppose that you accidentally cut a letter or enclosure as you are opening an envelope with a paper knife. 5.____
   The one of the following that you should do FIRST is to

   A. determine whether the document is important
   B. clip or staple the pieces together and process as usual
   C. mend the cut document with transparent tape
   D. notify the sender that the communication was damaged and request another copy

6. As soon as you pick up the phone, a very angry caller begins immediately to complain about city agencies and *red tape*. He says that he has been shifted to two or three different offices. It turns out that he is seeking information which is not immediately available to you. You believe you know, however, where it can be found. 6.____
Which of the following actions is the BEST one for you to take?

   A. To eliminate all confusion, suggest that the caller write the mayor stating explicitly what he wants.
   B. Apologize by telling the caller how busy city agencies now are, but also tell him directly that you do not have the information he needs.
   C. Ask for the caller's telephone number, and assure him you will call back after you have checked further.
   D. Give the caller the name and telephone number of the person who might be able to help, but explain that you are not positive he will get results.

7. Suppose that one of your duties is to dictate responses to routine requests from the public for information. A letter writer asks for information which, as expressed in a one-sentence, explicit agency rule, cannot be given out to the public. 7.____
Of the following ways of answering the letter, which is the MOST efficient?

   A. Quote verbatim that section of the agency rules which prohibits giving this information to the public.
   B. Without quoting the rule, explain why you cannot accede to the request and suggest alternative sources.
   C. Describe how carefully the request was considered before classifying it as subject to the rule forbidding the issuance of such information.
   D. Acknowledge receipt of the letter and advise that the requested information is not released to the public.

8. Suppose you assist in supervising a staff which has rather high morale, and your own supervisor asks you to poll the staff to find out who will be able to work overtime this particular evening to help complete emergency work. 8.____
Which of the following approaches would be MOST likely to win their cooperation while maintaining their morale?

   A. Tell them that the better assignments will be given only to those who work overtime.
   B. Tell them that occasional overtime is a job requirement.
   C. Assure them they'll be doing you a personal favor.
   D. Let them know clearly why the overtime is needed.

9. Suppose that you have been asked to write and to prepare for reproduction new departmental vacation leave regulations. 9.____
After you have written the new regulations, all of which fit on two pages, which one of the following would be the BEST method of reproducing 1,000 copies?

   A. An outside private printer because you can best maintain confidentiality using this technique
   B. Photocopying because the copies will have the best possible appearance
   C. Sending the file to all department employees as printable PDFs
   D. Printing and collating on the office high-volume printer

10. You are in charge of verifying employees' qualifications. This involves telephoning previous employers and schools. One of the applications which you are reviewing contains information which you are almost certain is correct on the basis of what the employee has told you.
The BEST thing to do is to 10.____

A. check the information again with the employer
B. perform the required verification procedures
C. accept the information as valid
D. ask a superior to verify the information

11. The practice of immediately identifying oneself and one's place of employment when contacting persons on the telephone is 11.____

A. *good* because the receiver of the call can quickly identify the caller and establish a frame of reference
B. *good* because it helps to set the caller at ease with the other party
C. *poor* because it is not necessary to divulge that information when making general calls
D. *poor* because it takes longer to arrive at the topic to be discussed

12. Which one of the following should be the MOST important overall consideration when preparing a recommendation to automate a large-scale office activity?
The 12.____

A. number of models of automated equipment available
B. benefits and costs of automation
C. fears and resistance of affected employees
D. experience of offices which have automated similar activities

13. A tickler file is MOST appropriate for filing materials 13.____

A. chronologically according to date they were received
B. alphabetically by name
C. alphabetically by subject
D. chronologically according to date they should be followed up

14. Which of the following is the BEST reason for decentralizing rather then centralizing the use of duplicating machines? 14.____

A. Developing and retaining efficient duplicating machine operators
B. Facilitating supervision of duplicating services
C. Motivating employees to produce legible duplicated copies
D. Placing the duplicating machines where they are most convenient and most frequently used

15. Window envelopes are sometimes considered preferable to individually addressed envelopes PRIMARILY because 15.____

A. window envelopes are available in standard sizes for all purposes
B. window envelopes are more attractive and official-looking
C. the use of window envelopes eliminates the risk of inserting a letter in the wrong envelope
D. the use of window envelopes requires neater typing

16. In planning the layout of a new office, the utilization of space and the arrangement of staff, furnishings, and equipment should usually be MOST influenced by the 16.____

A. gross square footage
B. status differences in the chain of command
C. framework of informal relationships among employees
D. activities to be performed

17. Office forms sometimes consist of several copies, each of a different color. The MAIN reason for using different colors is to 17.____

A. make a favorable impression on the users of the form
B. distinguish each copy from the others
C. facilitate the preparation of legible carbon copies
D. reduce cost, since using colored stock permits recycling of paper

18. Which of the following is the BEST justification for obtaining a photocopying machine for the office? 18.____

A. A photocopying machine can produce an unlimited number of copies at a low fixed cost per copy.
B. Employees need little training in operating a photocopying machine.
C. Office costs will be reduced and efficiency increased.
D. The legibility of a photocopy generally is superior to copy produced by any other office duplicating device.

19. An administrative officer in charge of a small fund for buying office supplies has just written a check to Charles Laird, a supplier, and has sent the check by messenger to him. A half-hour later, the messenger telephones the administrative officer. He has lost the check.
Which of the following is the MOST important action for the administrative officer to take under these circumstances? 19.____

A. Ask the messenger to return and write a report describing the loss of the check.
B. Make a note on the performance record of the messenger who lost the check.
C. Take the necessary steps to have payment stopped on the check.
D. Refrain from doing anything since the check may be found shortly.

20. A petty cash fund is set up PRIMARILY to 20.____

A. take care of small investments that must be made from time to time
B. take care of small expenses that arise from time to time
C. provide a fund to be used as the office wants to use it with little need to maintain records
D. take care of expenses that develop during emergencies such as machine breakdowns and fires

21. Your superior has asked you to send a package from your agency to a government agency in another city. He has written out the message and has indicated the name of the government agency.
When you prepare the package for mailing, which of the following items that your superior has not mentioned must you be sure to include? 21.____

A. Today's date
B. The full address of the government agency
C. A polite opening such as *Dear Sirs*
D. A final sentence such as *We would appreciate hearing from your agency in reply as soon as is convenient for you*

22. In addition to the original piece of correspondence, one should USUALLY also have typed 22.____

A. a single copy
B. as many copies as can be typed at one time
C. no more copies than are needed
D. two copies

23. The one of the following which is the BEST procedure to follow when making a short insert in a completed dictation is to 23.____

A. label the insert with a letter and indicate the position of the insert in the text by writing the identifying letter in the proper place
B. squeeze the insert into its proper place within the main text of the dictation
C. take down the insert and check the placement with the person who dictated when you are ready to transcribe your notes
D. transcribe the dictation into longhand, including the insert in its proper position

24. The one of the following procedures which will be MOST efficient in helping you to quickly open your dictation notebook to a clean sheet is to 24.____

A. clip or place a rubberband around the used portion of the notebook
B. leave the book out and open to a clean page when not in use
C. transcribe each dictation after it is given and rip out the used pages
D. use a book marker to indicate which portion of the notebook has been used

25. The purpose of dating your dictation notebooks is GENERALLY to 25.____

A. enable you to easily refer to your notes at a later date
B. ensure that you transcribe your notes in the order in which they were dictated
C. set up a precise record-keeping procedure
D. show your employer that you pay attention to detail

KEY (CORRECT ANSWERS)

1. C
2. B
3. C
4. C
5. C
6. C
7. A
8. D
9. D
10. B
11. A
12. B
13. D
14. D
15. C
16. D
17. B
18. C
19. C
20. B
21. B
22. C
23. A
24. A
25. A

TEST 2

DIRECTIONS: Each question or incomplete statement is followed by several suggested answers or completions. Select the one that BEST answers the question or completes the statement. *PRINT THE LETTER OF THE CORRECT ANSWER IN THE SPACE AT THE RIGHT.*

1. With regard to typed correspondence received by most offices, which of the following is the GREATEST problem? 1.____

   A. Verbosity
   B. Illegibility
   C. Improper folding
   D. Excessive copies

2. Of the following, the GREATEST advantage of flash drives over rewritable CD storage is that they 2.____

   A. are portable
   B. are both smaller and lighter
   C. contain more storage space
   D. allow files to be deleted to free space

3. Suppose that a large quantity of information is in the files which are located a good distance from your desk. Almost every worker in your office must use these files constantly. Your duties in particular require that you daily refer to about 25 of the same items. They are short, one-page items distributed throughout the files. In this situation, your BEST course would be to 3.____

   A. take the items that you use daily from the files and keep them on your desk, inserting *out cards* in their place
   B. go to the files each time you need the information so that the items will be there when other workers need them
   C. make xerox copies of the information you use most frequently and keep them in your desk for ready reference
   D. label the items you use most often with different colored tabs for immediate identification

4. Of the following, the MOST important advantage of preparing manuals of office procedures in loose-leaf form is that this form 4.____

   A. permits several employees to use different sections simultaneously
   B. facilitates the addition of new material and the removal of obsolete material
   C. is more readily arranged in alphabetical order
   D. reduces the need for cross-references to locate material carried under several headings

5. Suppose that you establish a new clerical procedure for the unit you supervise. Your keeping a close check on the time required by your staff to handle the new procedure is WISE mainly because such a check will find out 5.____

   A. whether your subordinates know how to handle the new procedure
   B. whether a revision of the unit's work schedule will be necessary as a result of the new procedure
   C. what attitude your employees have toward the new procedure
   D. what alterations in job descriptions will be necessitated by the new procedure

6. The numbered statements below relate to the stenographic skill of taking dictation. According to authorities on secretarial practices, which of these are generally recommended guides to development of efficient stenographic skills? 6.____

STATEMENTS

1. A stenographer should date her notebook daily to facilitate locating certain notes at a later time.
2. A stenographer should make corrections of grammatical mistakes while her boss is dictating to her.
3. A stenographer should draw a line through the dictated matter in her notebook after she has transcribed it.
4. A stenographer should write in longhand unfamiliar names and addresses dictated to her.

The CORRECT answer is:

A. Only Statements 1, 2, and 3 are generally recommended guides.
B. Only Statements 2, 3, and 4 are generally recommended guides.
C. Only Statements 1, 3, and 4 are generally recommended guides.
D. All four statements are generally recommended guides.

7. According to generally recognized rules of filing in an alphabetic filing system, the one of the following names which normally should be filed LAST is 7.____

A. Department of Education, New York State
B. F.B.I.
C. Police Department of New York City
D. P.S. 81 of New York City

8. Which one of the following forms for the typed name of the dictator in the closing lines of a letter is generally MOST acceptable in the United States? 8.____

A. (Dr.) James F. Fenton
B. Dr. James F. Fenton
C. Mr. James F. Fenton, Ph.D.
D. James F. Fenton

9. Which of the following is, MOST generally, a rule to be followed when typing a rough draft? 9.____

A. The copy should be single spaced.
B. The copy should be triple spaced.
C. There is no need for including footnotes.
D. Errors must be neatly corrected.

10. An office assistant needs a synonym.
Of the following, the book which she would find MOST useful is 10.____

A. a world atlas
B. BARTLETT'S FAMILIAR QUOTATIONS
C. a manual of style
D. a thesaurus

11. Of the following examples of footnotes, the one that is expressed in the MOST generally accepted standard form is: 11.____

    A. Johnson, T.F. (Dr.), English for Everyone, 3rd or 4th edition; New York City Linton Publishing Company, p. 467
    B. Frank Taylor, English for Today (New York: Rayton Publishing Company, 1971), p. 156
    C. Ralph Wilden, English for Tomorrow, Reynolds Publishing Company, England, p. 451
    D. Quinn, David, Yesterday's English (New York: Baldwin Publishing Company, 1972), p. 431

12. Standard procedures are used in offices PRIMARILY because 12.____

    A. an office is a happier place if everyone is doing the tasks in the same manner
    B. particular ways of doing jobs are considered more efficient than other ways
    C. it is good discipline for workers to follow standard procedures approved by the supervisor
    D. supervisors generally don't want workers to be creative in planning their work

13. Assume that an office assistant has the responsibility for compiling, typing, and mailing a preliminary announcement of Spring term course offerings. The announcement will go to approximately 900 currently enrolled students. Assuming that the following equipment is available for use, the MOST EFFECTIVE method for distributing the announcement to all 900 students is to 13.____

    A. e-mail it as a text document using the electronic student mailing list
    B. post the announcement as a PDF document for download on the department website
    C. send it by fax
    D. post the announcement and leave copies in buildings around campus

14. *Justified typing* is a term that refers MOST specifically to typewriting copy 14.____

    A. that has been edited and for which final copy is being prepared
    B. in a form that allows for an even right-hand margin
    C. with a predetermined vertical placement for each alternate line
    D. that has been approved by the supervisor and his superior

15. Which one of the following is the BEST form for the address in a letter? 15.____

    A. Mr. John Jones
       Vice President, The Universal Printing Company
       1220 Fifth Avenue
       New York, 10023 New York
    B. Mr. John Jones, Vice President
       The Universal Printing Company
       1220 Fifth Avenue
       New York, New York 10023
    C. Mr. John Jones, Vice President, The Universal Printing Company
       1220 Fifth Avenue
       New York, New York 10023

D. Mr. John Jones Vice President,
The Universal Printing Company
1220 Fifth Avenue
New York, 10023 New York

16. Of the following, the CHIEF advantage of the use of window envelopes over ordinary envelopes is that window envelopes 16.____

A. eliminate the need for addressing envelopes
B. protect the confidential nature of enclosed material
C. cost less to buy than ordinary envelopes
D. reduce the danger of the address becoming illegible

17. In the complimentary close of a business letter, the FIRST letter of ________ should be capitalized. 17.____

A. all the words
B. none of the words
C. only the first word
D. only the last word

18. Assume that one of your duties is to procure needed office supplies from the supply room. You are permitted to draw supplies every two weeks. 18.____
The one of the following which would be the MOST desirable practice for you to follow in obtaining supplies is to

A. obtain a quantity of supplies sufficient to last for several months to make certain that enough supplies are always on hand
B. determine the minimum supply necessary to keep on hand for the various items and obtain an additional quantity as soon as possible after the supply on hand has been reduced to this minimum
C. review the supplies once a month to determine what items have been exhausted and obtain an additional quantity as soon as possible
D. obtain a supply of an item as soon after it has been exhausted as is possible

19. Some offices that keep carbon copies of letters use several different colors of carbon paper for making carbon copies. 19.____
Of the following, the CHIEF reason for using different colors of carbon paper is to

A. facilitate identification of different types of letters in the files
B. relieve the monotony of typing and filing carbon copies
C. reduce the costs of preparing carbon copies
D. utilize both sides of the carbon paper for typing

20. Your supervisor asks you to post an online ad for freelance designers interested in submitting samples for a new company logo. Prospective workers should be proficient in which of the following software? 20.____

A. Microsoft Word
B. Adobe Acrobat Pro
C. Adobe Illustrator
D. Microsoft PowerPoint

21. Gary Thompson is applying for a position with the firm of Gray and Williams. Which letter should be filed in top position in the *Application* folder? 21.____

A. A letter of recommendation written on September 18 by Johnson & Smith
B. Williams' letter of October 8 requesting further details regarding Thompson's experience

C. Thompson's letter of September 8 making application for a position as sales manager
D. Letter of September 20 from Alfred Jackson recommending Thompson for the job

22. The USUAL arrangement in indexing the names of the First National Bank, Toledo, is 22.____

A. First National Bank, Toledo, Ohio
B. Ohio, First National Bank, Toledo
C. Toledo, First National Bank, Ohio
D. Ohio, Toledo, First National Bank

23. A single line through typed text indicating that it's incorrect or invalid is known as a(n) 23.____

A. underline
B. strikethrough
C. line font
D. eraser

24. A typical e-mail with an attachment should contain all of the following for successful transmittal EXCEPT 24.____

A. recipient's address
B. file attachment
C. body text
D. description of attachment

25. The subject line in a letter is USUALLY typed a ______ space below the ______. 25.____

A. single; inside address
B. single; salutation
C. double; inside address
D. double; salutation

KEY (CORRECT ANSWERS)

1. A
2. C
3. C
4. B
5. B
6. C
7. D
8. D
9. B
10. D
11. B
12. B
13. A
14. B
15. B
16. A
17. C
18. B
19. A
20. C
21. B
22. A
23. B
24. D
25. D

EXAMINATION SECTION
TEST 1

DIRECTIONS: Each question or incomplete statement is followed by several suggested answers or completions. Select the one that BEST answers the question or completes the statement. *PRINT THE LETTER OF THE CORRECT ANSWER IN THE SPACE AT THE RIGHT.*

Questions 1-22.

DIRECTIONS: Read through each group of words. Indicate in the space at the right the letter of the misspelled word.

1. A. miniature B. recession C. accommodate D. supress 1._____

2. A. mortgage B. illogical C. fasinate D. pronounce 2._____

3. A. calendar B. heros C. ecstasy D. librarian 3._____

4. A. initiative B. extraordinary C. villian D. exaggerate 4._____

5. A. absence B. sense C. dosn't D. height 5._____

6. A. curiosity B. ninety C. truely D. grammar 6._____

7. A. amateur B. definate C. meant D. changeable 7._____

8. A. excellent B. studioes C. achievement D. weird 8._____

9. A. goverment B. description C. sergeant D. desirable 9._____

10. A. proceed B. anxious C. neice D. precede 10._____

11. A. environment B. omitted C. apparant D. misconstrue 11._____

12. A. comparative B. hindrance C. benefited D. unamimous 12._____

13. A. embarrass B. recommend C. desciple D. argument 13._____

14. A. sophomore B. superintendent C. concievable D. disastrous 14._____

15. A. agressive B. questionnaire 15.____
C. occurred D. rhythm

16. A. peaceable B. conscientious 16.____
C. redicule D. deterrent

17. A. mischievious B. writing 17.____
C. competition D. athletics

18. A. auxiliary B. synonymous 18.____
C. maneuver D. repitition

19. A. existence B. optomistic 19.____
C. acquitted D. tragedy

20. A. hypocrisy B. parrallel 20.____
C. exhilaration D. prevalent

21. A. convalesence B. infallible 21.____
C. destitute D. grotesque

22. A. magnanimity B. asassination 22.____
C. incorrigible D. pestilence

Questions 23-40.

DIRECTIONS: In Questions 23 through 40, one sentence fragment contains an error in punctuation or capitalization. Indicate the letter of the INCORRECT sentence fragment and place it in space at the right.

23. A. Despite a year's work 23.____
B. in a well-equipped laboratory,
C. my Uncle failed to complete his research;
D. now he will never graduate.

24. A. Gene, if you are going to sleep 24.____
B. all afternoon I will enter
C. that ladies' golf tournament
D. sponsored by the Chamber of Commerce.

25. A. Seeing the cat slink toward the barn, 25.____
B. the farmer's wife jumped off the
C. ladder picked up a broom, and began
D. shouting at the top of her voice.

26. A. Extending over southeast Idaho and 26.____
B. northwest Wyoming, the Tetons
C. are noted for their height; however the
D. highest peak is actually under 14,000 feet.

27. A. "Sarah, can you recall the name 27.____
B. of the English queen
C. who supposedly said, 'We are not
D. amused?"

28. A. My aunt's graduation present to me 28.____
B. cost, I imagine more than she could
C. actually afford. It's a
D. Swiss watch with numerous features.

29. A. On the left are examples of buildings 29.____
B. from the Classical Period; two temples
C. one of which was dedicated to Zeus; the
D. Agora, a marketplace; and a large arch.

30. A. Tired of sonic booms, the people who 30.____
B. live near Springfield's Municipal Airport
C. formed an anti noise organization
D. with the amusing name of Sound Off.

31. A. "Joe, Mrs. Sweeney said, "your family 31.____
B. arrives Sunday. Since you'll be in
C. the Labor Day parade, we could ask Mr.
D. Krohn, who has a big car, to meet them."

32. A. The plumber emerged from the basement and 32.____
B. said, "Mr. Cohen I found the trouble in
C. your water heater. Could you move those
D. Schwinn bikes out of my way?"

33. A. The President walked slowly to the 33.____
B. podium, bowed to Edward Everett Hale
C. the other speaker, and began his formal address:
D. "Fourscore and seven years ago...."

34. A. Mr. Fontana, I hope, will arrive before 34.____
B. the beginning of the ceremonies; however,
C. if his plane is delayed, I have a substitute
D. speaker who can be here at a moments' notice.

35. A. Gladys wedding dress, a satin creation, 35.____
B. lay crumpled on the floor; her veil,
C. torn and streaked, lay nearby. "Jilted!"
D. shrieked Gladys. She was clearly annoyed.

36. A. Although it is poor grammar, the word 36.____
B. hopefully has become television's newest
C. pet expression; I hope (to use the correct
D. form) that it will soon pass from favor.

37. A. Plaza Apartment Hotel 37.____
B. 103 Tower road
C. Hampstead, Iowa 52025
D. March 13, 2008

38. A. Circulation Department 38.____
B. British History Illustrated
C. 3000 Walnut Street
D. Boulder Colorado 80302

39. A. Dear Sirs: 39.____
B. Last spring I ordered a subscription to your
C. magazine. I had read and enjoyed the May
D. issue containing the article titled "kings."

40. A. I have not however, received a 40.____
B. single issue. Will you check this?
C. Sincerely,
D. Maria Herrera

Questions 41-70.

DIRECTIONS: Questions 41 through 70 represent common grammatical concerns: subject-verb agreement, appropriate use of pronouns, and appropriate use of verbs. Read each sentence and indicate the letter of the grammatically CORRECT answer in the space at the right.

41. THE REIVERS, one of William Faulkner's last works, _____ made into a movie starring Steve McQueen. 41.____

A. has been B. have been
C. are being D. were

42. He _____ on the ground, his eyes fastened on an ant slowly pushing a morsel of food toward the ant hill. 42.____

A. layed B. laid C. had laid D. lay

43. Nobody in the tri-cities _____ to admit that a flood could be disastrous. 43.____

A. are willing B. have been willing
C. is willing D. were willing

44. "_____," the senator asked, "have you convinced to run against the incumbent?" 44.____

A. Who B. Whom C. Whomever D. Whomsoever

45. Of all the psychology courses that I took, Statistics 101 _____ the most demanding. 45.____

A. was B. are C. is D. were

46. Neither the conductor nor the orchestra members ______ the music to be applauded so enthusiastically. 46.____

A. were expecting
B. was expecting
C. is expected
D. has been expecting

47. The requirements for admission to the Lettermen's Club ______ posted outside the athletic director's office for months. 47.____

A. was
B. was being
C. has been
D. have been

48. Please give me a list of the people ______ to compete in the kayak race. 48.____

A. whom you think have planned
B. who you think has planned
C. who you think is planning
D. who you think are planning

49. I saw Eloise and Abelard earlier today; ______ were riding around in a fancy 1956 MG. 49.____

A. she and him
B. her and him
C. she and he
D. her and he

50. If you ______ the trunk in the attic, I'll unpack it later today. 50.____

A. can sit
B. are able to sit
C. can set
D. have sat

51. ______ all of the flour been used, or may I borrow three cups? 51.____

A. Have B. Has C. Is D. Could

52. In exasperation, the cycle shop's owner suggested that ______ there too long. 52.____

A. us boys were
B. we boys were
C. us boys had been
D. we boys had been

53. Idleness as well as money ______ the root of all evil. 53.____

A. have been
B. were to have been
C. is
D. are

54. Only the string players from the quartet – Gregory, Isaac, ______ - remained after the concert to answer questions. 54.____

A. him, and I
B. he, and I
C. him, and me
D. he, and me

55. Of all the antiques that ______ for sale, Gertrude chose to buy a stupid glass thimble. 55.____

A. was
B. is
C. would have
D. were

56. The detective snapped, "Don't confuse me with theories about ______ you believe committed the crime!" 56.____

A. who B. whom C. whomever D. which

57. _______ when we first called, we might have avoided our present predicament. 57.____

A. The plumber's coming
B. If the plumber would have come
C. If the plumber had come
D. If the plumber was to have come

58. We thought the sun ______ in the north until we discovered that our compass was defective. 58.____

A. had rose
B. had risen
C. had rised
D. had raised

59. Each play of Shakespeare's ______ more than ______ share of memorable characters. 59.____

A. contain; its
B. contains; its
C. contains; it's
D. contain; their

60. Our English teacher suggested to ______ seniors that either Tolstoy or Dickens ______ the outstanding novelist of the nineteenth century. 60.____

A. we; was considered
B. we; were considered
C. us; was considered
D. us; were considered

61. Sherlock Holmes, together with his great friend and companion Dr. Watson, ______ to aid the woman ______ had stumbled into the room. 61.____

A. has agreed; who
B. have agreed; whom
C. has agreed; whom
D. have agreed; who

62. Several of the deer ______ when they spotted my backpack ______ open in the meadow. 62.____

A. was frightened; laying
B. were frightened; lying
C. were frightened; laying
D. was frightened; lying

63. After the Scholarship Committee announces ______ selection, hysterics often ______. 63.____

A. it's; occur
B. its; occur
C. their; occur
D. their; occurs

64. I ______ the key on the table last night so you and ______ could find it. 64.____

A. layed; her
B. lay; she
C. laid; she
D. laid; her

65. Some of the antelope ______ wandered away from the meadow where the rancher ______ the block of salt. 65.____

A. has; sat
B. has; set
C. have; had set
D. has; sets

66. Macaroni and cheese ______ best to us (that is, to Andy and ______) when Mother adds extra cheddar cheese. 66.____

A. tastes; I
B. tastes; me
C. taste; me
D. taste; I

67. Frank said, "It must have been ______ called the phone company." 67.____

A. she who
B. she whom
C. her who
D. her whom

68. The herd ______ moving restlessly at every bolt of lightning; it was either Ted or ______ who saw the beginning of the stampede. 68.____

A. was; me
B. were; I
C. was; I
D. have been; me

69. The foreman ______ his lateness by saying that his alarm clock ______ until six minutes before eight. 69.____

A. explains; had not rang
B. explained; has not rung
C. has explained; rung
D. explained; hadn't rung

70. Of all the coaches, Ms. Cox is the only one who ______ that Sherry dives more gracefully than ______. 70.____

A. is always saying; I
B. is always saying; me
C. are always saying; I
D. were always saying; me

Questions 71-90.

DIRECTIONS: Choose the word in Questions 71 through 90 that is MOST opposite in meaning to the italicized word.

71. *fact* 71.____

A. statistic
B. statement
C. incredible
D. conjecture

72. *stiff* 72.____

A. fastidious
B. babble
C. supple
D. apprehensive

73. *blunt* 73.____

A. concise
B. tactful
C. artistic
D. humble

74. *foreign* 74.____

A. pertinent
B. comely
C. strange
D. scrupulous

75. *anger* 75.____

A. infer
B. pacify
C. taint
D. revile

76. *frank* 76.____

A. earnest
B. reticent
C. post
D. expensive

77. *secure* 77.____

A. precarious B. acquire C. moderate D. frenzied

78. *petty* 78.____

A. harmonious B. careful C. forthright D. momentous

79. *concede* 79.____

A. dispute B. reciprocate
C. subvert D. propagate

80. *benefit* 80.____

A. liquidation B. bazaar
C. detriment D. profit

81. *capricious* 81.____

A. preposterous B. constant
C. diabolical D. careless

82. *boisterous* 82.____

A. devious B. valiant C. girlish D. taciturn

83. *harmony* 83.____

A. congruence B. discord C. chagrin D. melody

84. *laudable* 84.____

A. auspicious B. despicable
C. acclaimed D. doubtful

85. *adherent* 85.____

A. partisan B. stoic C. renegade D. recluse

86. *exuberant* 86.____

A. frail B. corpulent C. austere D. bigot

87. *spurn* 87.____

A. accede B. flail
C. efface D. annihilate

88. *spontaneous* 88.____

A. hapless B. corrosive
C. intentional D. willful

89. *disparage* 89.____

A. abolish B. exude C. incriminate D. extol

90. *timorous* 90.____

A. succinct B. chaste
C. audacious D. insouciant

KEY (CORRECT ANSWERS)

1.	D	21.	A	41.	A	61.	A	81.	B
2.	C	22.	B	42.	D	62.	B	82.	D
3.	B	23.	C	43.	C	63.	B	83.	B
4.	C	24.	B	44.	B	64.	C	84.	B
5.	C	25.	C	45.	A	65.	C	85.	C
6.	C	26.	C	46.	A	66.	B	86.	C
7.	B	27.	D	47.	D	67.	A	87.	A
8.	B	28.	B	48.	A	68.	C	88.	C
9.	A	29.	B	49.	C	69.	D	89.	D
10.	C	30.	C	50.	C	70.	A	90.	C
11.	C	31.	A	51.	B	71.	D		
12.	D	32.	B	52.	D	72.	C		
13.	C	33.	B	53.	C	73.	B		
14.	C	34.	D	54.	B	74.	A		
15.	A	35.	A	55.	D	75.	B		
16.	C	36.	B	56.	B	76.	B		
17.	A	37.	B	57.	C	77.	A		
18.	D	38.	D	58.	B	78.	D		
19.	B	39.	D	59.	B	79.	A		
20.	B	40.	A	60.	C	80.	C		

READING COMPREHENSION
UNDERSTANDING AND INTERPRETING WRITTEN MATERIAL

COMMENTARY

The ability to read and understand written materials – texts, publications, newspapers, orders, directions, expositions – is a skill basic to a functioning democracy and to an efficient business or viable government.

That is why almost all examinations – for beginning, middle, and senior levels – test reading comprehension, directly or indirectly.

The reading test measures how well you understand what you read. This is how it is done: You read a short paragraph and five statements. From the five statements, you choose the one statement, or answer, that is BEST supported by, or best matches, what is said in the paragraph.

SAMPLE QUESTIONS

DIRECTIONS: Each question has five suggested answers, lettered A, B, C, D, and E. Decide which one is the BEST answer. *PRINT THE LETTER OF THE CORRECT ANSWER IN THE SPACE AT THE RIGHT.*

1. The prevention of accidents makes it necessary not only that safety devices be used to guard exposed machinery but also that mechanics be instructed in safety rules which they must follow for their own protection and that the light in the plant be adequate. The paragraph BEST supports the statement that industrial accidents 1.____

   A. are always avoidable
   B. may be due to ignorance
   C. usually result from inadequate machinery
   D. cannot be entirely overcome
   E. result in damage to machinery

ANALYSIS

Remember what you have to do–

First - Read the paragraph.
Second - Decide what the paragraph means.
Third - Read the five suggested answers.
Fourth - Select the one answer which BEST matches what the paragraph says or is BEST supported by something in the paragraph. (Sometimes you may have to read the paragraph again in order to be sure which suggested answer is best.)

This paragraph is talking about three steps that should be taken to prevent industrial accidents–

1. use safety devices on machines
2. instruct mechanics in safety rules
3. provide adequate lighting.

SELECTION

With this in mind let's look at each suggested answer. Each one starts with "Industrial accidents..."

SUGGESTED ANSWER A.

Industrial accidents (A) are always avoidable.

(The paragraph talks about how to avoid accidents, but does not say that accidents are always avoidable.)

SUGGESTED ANSWER B.

Industrial accidents (b) may be due to ignorance.

(One of the steps given in the paragraph to prevent accidents is to instruct mechanics on safety rules. This suggests that lack of knowledge or ignorance of safety rules causes accidents. This suggested answer sounds like a good possibility for being the right answer.)

SUGGESTED ANSWER C.

Industrial accidents (C) usually result from inadequate machinery.

(The paragraph does suggest that exposed machines cause accidents, but it doesn't say that it is the usual cause of accidents. The word usually makes this a wrong answer.)

SUGGESTED ANSWER D.

Industrial accidents (D) cannot be entirely overcome.

(You may know from your own experience that this is a true statement. But that is not what the paragraph is talking about. Therefore it is NOT the correct answer.)

SUGGESTED ANSWER E.

Industrial accidents (E) result in damage to machinery.

(This is a statement that may or may not be true, but in any case it is NOT covered by the paragraph.)

Looking back, you see that the one suggested answer of the five given that BEST matches what the paragraph says is–

Industrial accidents (B) may be due to ignorance.

The CORRECT answer then is B.

Be sure you read ALL the possible answers before you make your choice. You may think that none of the five answers is really good, but choose the BEST one of the five.

---

2. Probably few people realize, as they drive on a concrete road, that steel is used to keep the surface flat in spite of the weight of the busses and trucks. Steel bars, deeply embedded in the concrete, provide sinews to take the stresses so that the stresses cannot crack the slab or make it wavy. 2.____
The paragraph BEST supports the statement that a concrete road

A. is expensive to build
B. usually cracks under heavy weights
C. looks like any other road
D. is used only for heavy traffic
E. is reinforced with other material

ANALYSIS

This paragraph is commenting on the fact that–

1. few people realize, as they drive on a concrete road, that steel is deeply embedded
2. steel keeps the surface flat
3. steel bars enable the road to take the stresses without cracking or becoming wavy.

SELECTION

Now read and think about the possible answers:

A. A concrete road is expensive to build. (Maybe so but that is not what the paragraph is about.)
B. A concrete road usually cracks under heavy weights. (The paragraph talks about using steel bars to prevent heavy weights from cracking concrete roads. It says nothing about how usual it is for the roads to crack. The word usually makes this suggested answer wrong.)
C. A concrete road looks like any other road. (This may or may not be true. The important thing to note is that it has nothing to do with what the paragraph is about.)
D. A concrete road is used only for heavy traffic. (This answer at least has something to do with the paragraph-concrete roads are used with heavy traffic but it does not say "used only.")
E. A concrete road is reinforced with other material. (This choice seems to be the correct one on two counts: First, the paragraph does suggest that concrete roads are made stronger by embedding steel bars in them. This is another way of saying "concrete roads are reinforced with steel bars." Second, by the process of elimination, the other four choices are ruled out as correct answers simply because they do not apply.)

You can be sure that not all the reading questions will be so easy as these.

HINTS FOR ANSWERING READING QUESTIONS

1. Read the paragraph carefully. Then read each suggested answer carefully. Read every word, because often one word can make the difference between a right and a wrong answer.
2. Choose that answer which is supported in the paragraph itself. Do not choose an answer which is a correct statement unless it is based on information in the paragraph.
3. Even though a suggested answer has many of the words used in the paragraph, it may still be wrong.
4. Look out for words – such as *always, never, entirely, or only* – which tend to make a suggested answer wrong.
5. Answer first those questions which you can answer most easily. Then work on the other questions.
6. If you can't figure out the answer to the question, guess.

READING COMPREHENSION
UNDERSTANDING WRITTEN MATERIALS

COMMENTARY

The ability to read and understand written materials – texts, publications, newspapers, orders, directions, expositions – is a skill basic to a functioning democracy and to an efficient business or viable government.

That is why almost all examinations – for beginning, middle, and senior levels – test reading comprehension, directly or indirectly.

The reading test measures how well you understand what you read. This is how it is done: You read a passage followed by several statements. From these statements, you choose the *one* statement, or answer, that is BEST supported by, or BEST matches, what is said in the paragraph. *PRINT THE LETTER OF THE CORRECT ANSWER IN THE SPACE AT THE RIGHT.*

SAMPLE QUESTION

DIRECTIONS: Answer Question 1 ONLY according to the information given in the following passage :

1. A cashier has to make many arithmetic calculations in connection with his work. Skill in arithmetic comes readily with practice; no special talent is needed. 1.____
   On the basis of the above statement, it is MOST accurate to state that

   A. the most important part of a cashier's job is to make calculations
   B. few cashiers have the special ability needed to handle arithmetic problems easily
   C. without special talent, cashiers cannot learn to do the calculations they are required to do in their work
   D. a cashier can, with practice, learn to handle the computations he is required to make.

   The *correct* answer is D.

EXAMINATION SECTION
TEST 1

Questions 1-5.

DIRECTIONS: Questions 1 to 5 are based on the following reading passage:

The size of each collection route will be determined by the amount of waste per stop, distance between stops, speed of loading, speed of truck, traffic conditions during loading time, etc.

Basically, the route should consist of a proper amount of work for a crew for the daily working period. The crew should service all properties eligible for this service in their area. Routes should, whenever practical, be compact, with a logical progression through the area. Unnecessary travel should be avoided. Traffic conditions on the route should be thoroughly studied to prevent lost time in loading, to reduce hazards to employees, and to minimize tying up of regular traffic movements by collection forces. Natural and physical barriers and arterial streets should be used as route boundaries wherever possible to avoid lost time in travel.

Routes within a district should be laid out so that the crews start at the point farthest from the disposal area and, as the day progresses, move toward that area, thus reducing the length of the haul. When possible, the work of the crews in a district should be parallel as they progress throughout the day, with routes finishing up within a short distance of each other. This enables the supervisor to be present when crews are completing their work and enables him to shift crews to trouble spots to complete the day's work.

1. Based on the above passage, an advantage of having collection routes end near one another is that 1.____

   A. routes can be made more compact
   B. unnecessary travel is avoided, saving manpower
   C. the length of the haul is reduced
   D. the supervisor can exercise better manpower control

2. Of the factors mentioned above which affect the size of a collection route, the two over which the sanitation forces have LEAST control are 2.____

   A. amount of waste; traffic conditions
   B. speed of loading; amount of waste
   C. speed of truck; distance between stops
   D. traffic conditions; speed of truck

3. According to the above passage, the size of a collection route is probably good if 3.____

   A. it is a fair day's work for a normal crew
   B. it is not necessary for the trucks to travel too fast
   C. the amount of waste collected can be handled properly
   D. the distance between stops is approximately equal

4. Based on the above passage, it is reasonable to assume that a sanitation officer laying out collection routes should NOT try to have 4.____

   A. an arterial street as a route boundary
   B. any routes near the disposal area
   C. the routes overlap a little
   D. the routes run in the same direction

5. The term "logical progression" as used in the second paragraph of the passage refers MOST nearly to 5.____

   A. collecting from street after street in order
   B. numbering streets one after the other
   C. rotating crew assignments
   D. using logic as a basis for assignment of crews

TEST 2

Questions 1-3.

DIRECTIONS: Answer Questions 1, 2, and 3 *SOLELY* on the basis of the paragraph below.

In an open discussion designed to arrive at solutions to community problems, the person leading the discussion group should give the members a chance to make their suggestions before he makes his. He must not be afraid of silence, if he talks just to keep things going, he will find he can't stop, and good discussion will not develop. In other words, the more he talks, the more the group will depend on him. If he finds, however, that no one seems ready to begin the discussion, his best "opening" is to ask for definitions of terms which form the basis of the discussion. By pulling out as many definitions or interpretations as possible, he can get the group started "thinking out loud," which is essential to good discussion.

1. According to the above paragraph, good group discussion is *most likely* to result if the person leading the discussion group 1.____

   A. keeps the discussion going by speaking whenever the group stops speaking
   B. encourages the group to depend on him by speaking more than any other group member
   C. makes his own suggestions before the group has a chance to make theirs
   D. encourages discussion by asking the group to interpret the terms to be discussed

2. According to the paragraph above, "thinking out loud" by the discussion group is 2.____

   A. *good* practice, because "thinking out loud" is important to good discussion
   B. *poor* practice, because group members should think out their ideas before discussing them
   C. *good* practice, because it will encourage the person leading the discussion to speak more
   D. *poor* practice, because it causes the group to fear silence during a discussion

3. According to the paragraph above, the *one* of the following which is LEAST desirable at an open discussion is having 3.____

   A. silent periods during which none of the group members speaks
   B. differences of opinion among the group members concerning the definition of terms
   C. a discussion leader who uses "openings" to get the discussion started
   D. a discussion leader who provides all suggestions and definitions for the group

---

TEST 3

Questions 1-4.

DIRECTIONS: Questions 1 through 4 are to be answered *SOLELY* on the basis of the following information.

The insects you will control are just a minute fraction of the millions which inhabit the world. Man does well to hold his own in the face of the constant pressures that insects continue to exert upon him. Not only are the total numbers tremendous, but the number of individual kinds, or species, certainly exceeds 800,000 – number greater than that of all other animals combined. Many of these are beneficial but some are especially competitive with man. Not only are insects numerous, but they are among he most adaptable of all animals. In their many forms, they are fitted for almost any specific way of life. Their adaptability, combined with their tremendous rate of reproduction, gives insects an unequaled potential for survival!

The food of insects includes almost anything that can be eaten by any other animal as well as many things which cannot even be digested by any other animals. Most insects do not harm the products of man or carry diseases harmful to him; however many do carry diseases and others feed on his food and manufactured goods. Some are adapted to living only in open areas while others are able to live in extremely confined spaces. All of these factors combined make the insects a group of animals having many members which are a nuisance to man and thus of great importance.

The control of insects requires an understanding of their way of life. Thus it is necessary to understand the anatomy of the insect, its method of growth, the time it takes for the insect to grow from egg to adult, its habits, the stage of its life history in which it causes damage, its food, and its common living places. In order to obtain the best control, it is especially important to be able to identify correctly the specific insect involved because, without this knowledge, it is impossible to prescribe a proper treatment.

1. Which one of the following is a CORRECT statement about the insect population of the world, according to the above paragraph? The — 1.____

   A. total number of insects is less than the total number of all other animals combined
   B. number of species of insects is greater than the number of species of all other animals combined
   C. total number of harmful insects is greater than the total number of those which are not harmful
   D. number of species of harmless insects is less than the number of species of those which are harmful

2. Insects will be controlled MOST efficiently if you — 2.____

   A. understand why the insects are so numerous
   B. know what insects you are dealing with
   C. see if the insects compete with man
   D. are able to identify the food which the insects digest

3. According to the above passage, insects are of importance to a scientist PRIMARILY because they 3.____

   A. can be annoying, destructive, and harmful to man
   B. are able to thrive in very small spaces
   C. cause damage during their growth stages
   D. are so adaptable that they can adjust to any environment

4. According to the above passage, insects can eat 4.____

   A. everything that any other living thing can eat
   B. man's food and things which he makes
   C. anything which other animals can't digest
   D. only food and food products

TEST 4

Questions 1-4.

DIRECTIONS: Answer Questions 1 through 4 on the basis of the information given in the following passage.

Telephone service in a government agency should be adequate and complete with respect to information given or action taken. It must be remembered that telephone contacts should receive special consideration since the caller cannot see the operator. People like to feel that they are receiving personal attention and that their requests or criticisms are receiving individual rather than routine consideration. All this contributes to what has come to be known as *tone of service*. The aim is to use standards which are clearly very good or superior. The factors to be considered in determining what makes good tone of service are speech, courtesy, understanding and explanations. A caller's impression of tone of service will affect the general public attitude toward the agency and city services in general.

1. The above passage states that people who telephone a government agency like to feel that they are 1.____

   A. creating a positive image of themselves
   B. being given routine consideration
   C. receiving individual attention
   D. setting standards for telephone service

2. Which of the following is NOT mentioned in the above passage as a factor in determining good tone of service? 2.____

   A. Courtesy B. Education C. Speech D. Understanding

3. The above passage implies that failure to properly handle telephone calls is *most likely* to result in 3.____

   A. a poor impression of city agencies by the public
   B. a deterioration of courtesy toward operators
   C. an effort by operators to improve the Tone of Service
   D. special consideration by the public of operator difficulties

TEST 5

Questions 1-5.

DIRECTIONS: Answer Questions 1 through 5 only on the basis of the information provided in the following passage:

For some office workers it is useful to be familiar with the four main classes of domestic mail; for others it is essential. Each class has a different rate of postage and some have requirements concerning wrapping, sealing or special information to be placed on the package.

First-class mail, the class which may not be opened for postal inspection, includes letters, post cards, business reply cards, and other kinds of written matter. There are different rates for some of the kinds of cards which can be sent by first-class mail. The maximum weight for an item sent by first-class mail is 70 pounds. An item which is not letter size should be marked "First Class" on all sides.

Although office workers most often come into contact with first-class mail, they may find it helpful to know something about the other classes. Second-class mail is generally used for mailing newspapers and magazines. Publishers of these articles must meet certain U.S. Postal Service requirements in order to obtain a permit to use second-class mailing rates. Third-class mail, which must weigh less than 1 pound, includes printed materials and merchandise parcels. There are two rate structures for this class, a single-piece rate and a bulk rate. Fourth-class mail, also known as parcel post, includes packages weighing from one to 40 pounds. For more information about these classes of mail and the actual mailing rates, contact your local post office.

1. According to this passage, first-class mail is the only class which 1.____

   A. has a limit on the maximum weight of an item
   B. has different rates for items within the class
   C. may not be opened for postal inspection
   D. should be used by office workers

2. According to this passage, the one of the following items which may CORRECTLY be sent by fourth-class mail is a 2.____

   A. magazine weighing one-half pound
   B. package weighing one-half pound
   C. package weighing two pounds
   D. post card

3. According to this passage, there are different postage rates for 3.____

   A. a newspaper sent by second-class mail and a magazine sent by second-class mail
   B. each of the classes of mail
   C. each pound of fourth-class mail
   D. printed material sent by third-class mail and merchandise parcels sent by third-class mail

4. In order to send a newspaper by second-class mail, a publisher must 4.____

   A. have met certain postal requirements and obtained a permit
   B. indicate whether he wants to use the single-piece or the bulk rate
   C. make certain that the newspaper weighs less than one pound
   D. mark the newspaper "Second Class" on the top and bottom of the wrapper

5. Of the following types of information the one which is NOT mentioned in the passage is the 5.____

   A. class of mail to which parcel post belongs
   B. kinds of items which can be sent by each class of mail
   C. maximum weight for an item sent by fourth-class mail
   D. postage rate for each of the four classes of mail

TEST 6

Questions 1-5.

DIRECTIONS: Questions numbered 1 to 5 inclusive are to be answered in accordance with the following paragraph.

The thickness of insulation necessary for the most economical results varies with the steam temperature. The standard covering consists of 85 percent magnesia with 10 percent of long-fibre asbestos as a binder. Both matnesia and laminated asbestos-felt and other forms of mineral wool including glass wool are also used for heat insulation. The magnesia and laminated-asbestos coverings may be safely used at temperatures up to 600° F. Pipe insulation is applied in molded sections 3 feet long; the sections are attached to the pipe by means of galvanized iron wire or netting. Flanges and fittings can be insulated by direct application of magnesia cement to the metal without *reinforcement.* Insulation should always be maintained in good condition because it saves fuel. Routine maintenance of warm-pipe insulation should include prompt repair of damaged surfaces. Steam and hot-water leaks concealed by insulation will be difficult to detect. Underground steam or hot-water pipes are best insulated using a concrete trench with removable cover.

1. The word *reinforcement*, as used above, means, most nearly, 1.____

   A. resistance B. strengthening C. regulation D. removal

2. According to the above paragraph, magnesia and laminated asbestos coverings may be *safely* used at temperatures up to 2.____

   A. 800° F B. 720° F C. 675° F D. 600° F

3. According to the above paragraph, insulation should *always* be maintained in good condition because it 3.____

   A. is laminated
   B. saves fuel
   C. is attached to the pipe
   D. prevents leaks

4. According to the above paragraph, pipe insulation sections are attached to the pipe by means of 4.____

   A. binders
   B. mineral wool
   C. netting
   D. staples

5. According to the above paragraph, a leak in a hot-water pipe may be difficult to detect because, when insulation is used, the leak is 5.____

   A. underground
   B. hidden
   C. routine
   D. cemented

TEST 7

Questions 1-4.

DIRECTIONS: Questions 1 to 4 inclusive are to be answered *only* in accordance with the following paragraph.

Cylindrical surfaces are the most common form of finished surfaces found on machine parts, although flat surfaces are also very common; hence, many metal-cutting *processes* are for the purpose of producing either cylindrical or flat surfaces. The machines used for cylindrical or flat shapes may be, and often are, utilized also for forming the various irregular or special shapes required on many machine parts. Because of the prevalence of cylindrical and flat surfaces, the student of manufacturing practice should learn first about the machines and methods employed to produce these surfaces. The cylindrical surfaces may be internal as in holes and cylinders. Any one part may, of course, have cylindrical sections of different diameters and lengths and include flat ends or shoulders and, frequently, there is a threaded part or, possibly, some finished surface that is not circular in cross-section. The prevalence of cylindrical surfaces on machine parts explains why lathes are found in all machine shops. It is important to understand the various uses of the lathe because many of the operations are the same fundamentally as those performed on other types of machine tools.

1. According to the above paragraph, the *most common* form of finished surfaces found on machine parts is 1.____

   A. cylindrical B. elliptical
   C. flat D. square

2. According to the above paragraph, *any one* part of cylindrical surfaces may have 2.____

   A. chases B. shoulders C. keyways D. splines

3. According to the above paragraph, lathes are found in all machine shops because cylindrical surfaces on machine parts are 3.____

   A. scarce B. internal C. common D. external

4. As used in the above paragraph, the word *processes* means 4.____

   A. operations B. purposes C. devices D. tools

TEST 8

Questions 1-2.

DIRECTIONS: Questions 1 and 2 are to be answered in accordance with the following paragraph.

The principle of interchangeability requires manufacture to such specification that component parts of a device may be selected at random and assembled to fit and operate satisfactorily. Interchangeable manufacture, therefore, requires that parts be made to definite limits of error, and to fit gages instead of mating parts. Interchangeability does not necessarily involve a high degree of precision; stove lids, for example, are interchangeable but are not particularly accurate, and carriage bolts and nuts are not precision products but are completely interchangeable. Interchangeability may be employed in unit-production as well as mass-production systems of manufacture.

1. According to the above paragraph, in order for parts to be interchangeable, they must be 1.____

   A. precision-machined
   B. selectively-assembled
   C. mass-produced
   D. made to fit gages

2. According to the above paragraph, carriage bolts are interchangeable because they are 2.____

   A. precision-made
   B. sized to specific tolerances
   C. individually matched products
   D. produced in small units

KEY (CORRECT ANSWERS)

TEST 1	TEST 2	TEST 3	TEST 4	TEST 5	TEST 6	TEST 7	TEST 8
1. D	1. D	1. B	1. C	1. C	1. B	1. A	1. D
2. A	2. A	2. B	2. B	2. C	2. D	2. B	2. B
3. A	3. D	3. A	3. A	3. B	3. B	3. C	
4. C		4. B		4. A	4. C	4. A	
5. A				5. D	5. B		

NAME and NUMBER COMPARISONS

COMMENTARY

This test seeks to measure your ability and disposition to do a job carefully and accurately, your attention to exactness and preciseness of detail, your alertness and versatility in discerning similarities and differences between things, and your power in systematically handling written language symbols.

It is actually a test of your ability to do academic and/or clerical work, using the basic elements of verbal (qualitative) and mathematical (quantitative) learning – words <u>and</u> numbers.

EXAMINATION SECTION
TEST 1

<u>Tests 1-2</u>

DIRECTIONS: Questions 1 through 6 consist of sets of names and addresses. In each question, the name and address in Column II should be an exact copy of the name and address in Column I. *PRINT IN THE SPACE AT THE RIGHT THE LETTER:*

A. if there is a mistake only in the name
B. if there is a mistake only in the address
C. if there is a mistake in both name and address
D. if there is no mistake in either name or address

SAMPLE:

Michael Filbert 456 Reade Street New York, N.Y. 10013	Michael Filbert 645 Reade Street New York, N.Y. 10013

Since there is a mistake only in the address, the answer is B.

1.	Esta Wong 141 West 68 St. New York, N.Y. 10023	Esta Wang 141 West 68 St. New York, N.Y. 10023	1.____
2.	Dr. Alberto Grosso 3475 12th Avenue Brooklyn, N.Y. 11218	Dr. Alberto Grosso 3475 12th Avenue Brooklyn, N.Y. 11218	2.____
3.	Mrs. Ruth Bortlas 482 Theresa Ct. Far Rockaway, N.Y. 11691	Ms. Ruth Bortlas 482 Theresa Ct. Far Rockaway, N.Y. 11169	3.____
4.	Mr. and Mrs. Howard Fox 2301 Sedgwick Ave. Bronx, N.Y. 10468	Mr. and Mrs. Howard Fox 231 Sedgwick Ave. Bronx, N.Y. 10468	4.____
5.	Miss Marjorie Black 223 East 23 Street New York, N.Y. 10010	Miss Margorie Black 223 East 23 Street New York, N.Y. 10010	5.____

6.	Michelle Herman 806 Valley Rd. Old Tappan, N.J. 07675	Michelle Hermann 806 Valley Dr. Old Tappan, N.J. 07675	6.____

KEY (CORRECT ANSWERS)

1. A
2. D
3. C
4. B
5. A
6. C

TEST 2

DIRECTIONS: Questions 1 through 6 consist of sets of names and addresses. In each question, the name and address in Column II should be an exact copy of the name and address in Column I. *PRINT IN THE SPACE AT THE RIGHT THE LETTER:*

A. if there is a mistake only in the name
B. if there is a mistake only in the address
C. if there is a mistake in both name and address
D. if there is no mistake in either name or address

	Column I	Column II	
1.	Ms. Joan Kelly 313 Franklin Ave. Brooklyn, N.Y. 11202	Ms. Joan Kielly 318 Franklin Ave. Brooklyn, N.Y. 11202	1.____
2.	Mrs. Eileen Engel 47-24 86 Road Queens, N.Y. 11122	Mrs. Ellen Engel 47-24 86 Road Queens, N.Y. 11122	2.____
3.	Marcia Michaels 213 E. 81 St. New York, N.Y. 10012	Marcia Michaels 213 E. 81 St. New York, N.Y. 10012	3.____
4.	Rev. Edward J. Smyth 1401 Brandeis Street San Francisco, Calif. 96201	Rev. Edward J. Smyth 1401 Brandies Street San Francisco, Calif. 96201	4.____
5.	Alicia Rodriguez 24-68 81 St. Elmhurst, N.Y. 11122	Alicia Rodriquez 2468 81 St. Elmhurst, N.Y. 11122	5.____
6.	Ernest Eisemann 21 Columbia St. New York, N.Y. 10007	Ernest Eisermann 21 Columbia St. New York, N.Y. 10007	6.____

KEY (CORRECT ANSWERS)

1. C
2. A
3. D
4. B
5. C
6. A

TEST 3

DIRECTIONS: Questions 1 through 8 consist of names, locations and telephone numbers. In each question, the name, location and number in Column II should be an exact copy of the name, location and number in Column I. *PRINT IN THE SPACE AT THE RIGHT THE LETTER:*

A. if there is a mistake in one line only
B. if there is a mistake in two lines only
C. if there is a mistake in three lines only
D. if there are no mistakes in any of the lines

1.	Ruth Lang EAM Bldg., Room C101 625-2000, ext. 765	Ruth Lang EAM Bldg., Room C110 625-2000, ext. 765	1.____
2.	Anne Marie Ionozzi Investigations, Room 827 576-4000, ext. 832	Anna Marie Ionozzi Investigation, Room 827 566-4000, ext. 832	2.____
3.	Willard Jameson Fm C Bldg. Room 687 454-3010	Willard Jamieson Fm C Bldg. Room 687 454-3010	3.____
4.	Joanne Zimmermann Bldg. SW, Room 314 532-4601	Joanne Zimmermann Bldg. SW, Room 314 532-4601	4.____
5.	Carlyle Whetstone Payroll Division-A, Room 212A 262-5000, ext. 471	Caryle Whetstone Payroll Division-A, Room 212A 262-5000, ext. 417	5.____
6.	Kenneth Chiang Legal Council, Room 9745 (201) 416-9100, ext. 17	Kenneth Chiang Legal Counsel, Room 9745 (201) 416-9100, ext. 17	6.____
7.	Ethel Koenig Personnel Services Div, Rm 433 635-7572	Ethel Hoenig Personal Services Div, Rm 433 635-7527	7.____
8.	Joyce Ehrhardt Office of Administrator, Rm W56 387-8706	Joyce Ehrhart Office of Administrator, Rm W56 387-7806	8.____

KEY (CORRECT ANSWERS)

1. A
2. C
3. A
4. D
5. B
6. A
7. C
8. B

TEST 4

DIRECTIONS: Each of questions 1 through 10 gives the identification number and name of a person who has received treatment at a certain hospital. You are to choose the option (A, B, C or D) which has EXACTLY the same number and name as those given in the question.

SAMPLE:

123765 Frank Y. Jones

A. 123675 Frank Y. Jones
B. 123765 Frank T. Jones
C. 123765 Frank Y. Johns
D. 123765 Frank Y. Jones

The correct answer is D, because it is the only option showing the identification number and name exactly as they are in the sample question.

1. 754898 Diane Malloy 1.____

A. 745898 Diane Malloy
B. 754898 Dion Malloy
C. 754898 Diane Malloy
D. 754898 Diane Maloy

2. 661818 Ferdinand Figueroa 2.____

A. 661818 Ferdinand Figeuroa
B. 661618 Ferdinand Figueroa
C. 661818 Ferdnand Figueroa
D. 661818 Ferdinand Figueroa

3. 100101 Norman D. Braustein 3.____

A. 100101 Norman D. Braustein
B. 101001 Norman D. Braustein
C. 100101 Norman P. Braustien
D. 100101 Norman D. Bruastein

4. 838696 Robert Kittredge 4.____

A. 838969 Robert Kittredge
B. 838696 Robert Kittredge
C. 388696 Robert Kittredge
D. 838696 Robert Kittridge

5. 243716 Abraham Soletsky 5.____

A. 243716 Abrahm Soletsky
B. 243716 Abraham Solestky
C. 243176 Abraham Soletsky
D. 243716 Abraham Soletsky

6. 981121 Phillip M. Maas 6.____

A. 981121 Phillip M. Mass
B. 981211 Phillip M. Maas
C. 981121 Phillip M. Maas
D. 981121 Phillip N. Maas

7. 786556 George Macalusso 7.____

A. 785656 George Macalusso
B. 786556 George Macalusso
C. 786556 George Maculusso
D. 786556 George Macluasso

8. 639472 Eugene Weber 8.____

A. 639472 Eugene Weber
B. 639472 Eugene Webre
C. 693472 Eugene Weber
D. 639742 Eugene Weber

9. 724936 John J. Lomonaco 9.____

A. 724936 John J. Lomanoco
B. 724396 John L. Lomonaco
C. 724936 John J. Lomonaco
D. 724936 John J. Lamonaco

10. 899868 Michael Schnitzer 10.____

A. 899868 Micheal Schnitzer
B. 898968 Michael Schnizter
C. 899688 Michael Schnitzer
D. 899868 Michael Schnitzer

KEY (CORRECT ANSWERS)

1.	C	6.	C
2.	D	7.	B
3.	A	8.	A
4.	B	9.	C
5.	D	10.	D

NAME AND NUMBER CHECKING

EXAMINATION SECTION
TEST 1

DIRECTIONS: This test is designed to measure your speed/and accuracy. You are urged to work both quickly and accurately and to do correctly as many lists as you can in the time allowed. The test consists of lists of pairs of names and numbers. Count the number of IDENTICAL pairs in each list. Then, select the correct number, 1,2, 3, 4, or 5, and indicate your choice by circling the corresponding number on your answer paper. Two sample questions are presented for your guidance, together with the correct solutions.

SAMPLE QUESTIONS CIRCLE CORRECT ANSWER

SAMPLE LIST A

Adelphi College - Adelphia College	1 2 3 4 5
Braxton Corp. - Braxeton Corp.	
Wassaic State School - Wassaic State School	
Central Islip State Hospital - Central Isllip State Hospital	
Greenwich House - Greenwich House	

NOTE that there are only two correct pairs - Wassaic State School and Greenwich House. Therefore, the CORRECT answer is 2.

SAMPLE LIST B

78453694	- 78453684	1 2 3 4 5
784530	- 784530	
533	- 534	
67845	- 67845	
2368745	- 2368755	

NOTE that there are only two correct pairs - 784530 and 67845. Therefore, the CORRECT answer is 2.

LIST 1

Diagnostic Clinic	- Diagnostic Clinic	1 2 3 4 5
Yorkville Health	- Yorkville Health	
Meinhard Clinic	- Meinhart Clinic	
Corlears Clinic	- Carlears Clinic	
Tremont Diagnostic	- Tremont Diagnostic	

LIST 2

73526	- 73526	1 2 3 4 5
7283627198	- 7283627198	
627	- 637	
728352617283	- 728352617282	
6281	- 6281	

LIST			CIRCLE CORRECT ANSWER
LIST 3	Jefferson Clinic	- Jeffersen Clinic	1 2 3 4 5
	Mott Haven Center	- Mott Havan Center	
	Bronx Hospital	- Bronx Hospital	
	Montefiore Hospital	- Montifeore Hospital	
	Beth Isreal Hospital	- Beth Israel Hospital	
LIST 4	936271826	- 936371826	1 2 3 4 5
	5271	- 5291	
	82637192037	- 82637192037	
	527182	- 5271882	
	726354256	- 72635456	
LIST 5	Trinity Hospital	- Trinity Hospital	1 2 3 4 5
	Central Harlem	- Centrel Harlem	
	St. Luke's Hospital	- St. Lukes' Hospital	
	Mt.Sinai Hospital	- Mt.Sinia Hospital	
	N.Y.Dispensery	- N.Y.Dispensary	
LIST 6	725361552637	- 725361555637	1 2 3 4 5
	7526378	- 7526377	
	6975	- 6975	
	82637481028	- 82637481028	
	3427	- 3429	
LIST 7	Misericordia Hospital	- Miseracordia Hospital	1 2 3 4 5
	Lebonan Hospital	- Lebanon Hospital	
	Gouverneur Hospital	- Gouverner Hospital	
	German Polyclinic	- German Policlinic	
	French Hospital	- French Hospital	
LIST 8	8277364933251	- 827364933351	1 2 3 4 5
	63728	- 63728	
	367281	- 367281	
	62733846273	- 6273846293	
	62836	- 6283	
LIST 9	King's County Hospital	- Kings County Hospital	1 2 3 4 5
	St.Johns Long Island	- St.John's Long Island	
	Bellevue Hospital	- Bellvue Hospital	
	Beth David Hospital	- Beth David Hospital	
	Samaritan Hospital	- Samariton Hospital	

CIRCLE CORRECT ANSWER

LIST 10

62836454	- 62836455	1 2 3 4 5
42738267	- 42738369	
573829	- 573829	
738291627874	- 738291627874	
725	- 735	

LIST 11

Bloomingdal Clinic	- Bloomingdale Clinic	1 2 3 4 5
Communitty Hospital	- Community Hospital	
Metroplitan Hospital	- Metropoliton Hospital	
Lenox Hill Hospital	- Lonex Hill Hospital	
Lincoln Hospital	- Lincoln Hospital	

LIST 12

6283364728	- 6283648	1 2 3 4 5
627385	- 627383	
54283902	- 54283602	
63354	- 63354	
7283562781	- 7283562781	

LIST 13

Sydenham Hospital	- Sydanham Hospital	1 2 3 4 5
Roosevalt Hospital	- Roosevelt Hospital	
Vanderbilt Clinic	- Vanderbild Clinic	
Women's Hospital	- Woman's Hospital	
Flushing Hospital	- Flushing Hospital	

LIST 14

62738	- 62738	1 2 3 4 5
727355542321	- 72735542321	
263849332	- 263849332	
262837	- 263837	
47382912	- 47382922	

LIST 15

Episcopal Hospital	- Episcapal Hospital	1 2 3 4 5
Flower Hospital	- Flouer Hospital	
Stuyvesent Clinic	- Stuyvesant Clinic	
Jamaica Clinic	- Jamaica Clinic	
Ridgwood Clinic	- Ridgewood Clinic	

LIST 16

628367299	- 628367399	1 2 3 4 5
111	- 111	
118293304829	- 1182839489	
4448	- 4448	
333693678	- 333693678	

CIRCLE
CORRECT ANSWER

LIST 17

Arietta Crane Farm	- Areitta Crane Farm	1 2 3 4 5
Bikur Chilim Home	- Bikur Chilom Home	
Burke Foundation	- Burke Foundation	
Blythedale Home	- Blythdale Home	
Campbell Cottages	- Cambell Cottages	

LIST 18

32123	- 32132	1 2 3 4 5
273893326783	- 27389326783	
473829	- 473829	
7382937	- 7383937	
362890122332	- 36289012332	

LIST 19

Caraline Rest	- Caroline Rest	1 2 3 4 5
Loreto Rest	- Loretto Rest	
Edgewater Creche	- Edgwater Creche	
Holiday Farm	- Holiday Farm	
House of St. Giles	- House of st. Giles	

LIST 20

557286777	- 55728677	1 2 3 4 5
3678902	- 3678892	
1567839	- 1567839	
7865434712	- 7865344712	
9927382	- 9927382	

LIST 21

Isabella Home	- Isabela Home	1 2 3 4 5
James A. Moore Home	- James A. More Home	
The Robin's Nest	- The Roben's Nest	
Pelham Home	- Pelam Home	
St.Eleanora's Home	- St. Eleanora's Home	

LIST 22

273648293048	- 273648293048	1 2 3 4 5
334	- 334	
7362536478	- 7362536478	
7362819273	- 7362819273	
7362	- 7363	

LIST 23

St.Pheobe's Mission	- St.Phebe's Mission	1 2 3 4 5
Seaside Home	- Seaside Home	
Speedwell Society	- Speedwell Society	
Valeria Home	- Valera Home	
Wiltwyck	- Wildwyck	

CIRCLE
CORRECT ANSWER

LIST 24

63728	- 63738	1 2 3 4 5
63728192736	- 63728192738	
428	- 458	
62738291527	- 62738291529	
63728192	- 63728192	

LIST 25

McGaffin	- McGafin	1 2 3 4 5
David Ardslee	- David Ardslee	
Axton Supply	- Axeton Supply Co	
Alice Russell	- Alice Russell	
Dobson Mfg.Co.	- Dobsen Mfg. Co.	

KEY (CORRECT ANSWERS)

1. 3
2. 3
3. 1
4. 1
5. 1
6. 2
7. 1
8. 2
9. 1
10. 2
11. 1
12. 2
13. 1
14. 2
15. 1
16. 3
17. 1
18. 1
19. 1
20. 2
21. 1
22. 4
23. 2
24. 1
25. 2

TEST 2

DIRECTIONS: This test is designed to measure your speed and accuracy. You are urged to work both quickly and accurately and to do correctly as many lists as you can in the time allowed. The test consists of lists of pairs of names and numbers. Count the number of IDENTICAL pairs in each list. Then, select the correct number, 1, 2, 3, 4, or 5, and indicate your choice by circling the corresponding number on your answer paper. Two sample questions are presented for your guidance, together with the correct solutions.

CIRCLE CORRECT ANSWER

LIST 1

82637381028	- 82637281028	1 2 3 4 5
928	- 928	
72937281028	- 72937281028	
7362	- 7362	
927382615	- 927382615	

LIST 2

Albee Theatre	- Albee Theatre	1 2 3 4 5
Lapland Lumber Co.	- Laplund Lumber Co.	
Adelphi College	- Adelphi College	
Jones & Son Inc.	- Jones & Sons Inc.	
S.W.Ponds Co.	- S.W. Ponds Co.	

LIST 3

85345	- 85345	1 2 3 4 5
895643278	- 895643277	
726352	- 726353	
632685	- 632685	
7263524	- 7236524	

LIST 4

Eagle Library	- Eagle Library	1 2 3 4 5
Dodge Ltd.	- Dodge Co.	
Stromberg Carlson	- Stromberg Carlsen	
Clairice Ling	- Clairice Linng	
Mason Book Co.	- Matson Book Co.	

LIST 5

66273	- 66273	1 2 3 4 5
629	- 620	
7382517283	- 7382517283	
637281	- 639281	
2738261	- 2788261	

		CIRCLE CORRECT ANSWER
LIST 6		
Robert MacColl	- Robert McColl	1 2 3 4 5
Buick Motor	- Buck Motors	
Murray Bay & Co.Ltd.	- Murray Bay Co.Ltd.	
L.T. Ltyle	- L.T, Lyttle	
A.S. Landas	- A.S. Landas	
LIST 7		
627152637490	- 627152637490	1 2 3 4 5
73526189	- 73526189	
5372	- 5392	
63728142	- 63728124	
4783946	- 4783046	
LIST 8		
Tyndall Burke	- Tyndell Burke	1 2 3 4 5
W. Briehl	- W, Briehl	
Burritt Publishing Co.	- Buritt Publishing Co.	
Frederick Breyer & Co.	- Frederick Breyer Co.	
Bailey Buulard	- Bailey Bullard	
LIST 9		
634	- 634	1 2 3 4 5
162837	- 163837	
273892223678	- 27389223678	
527182	- 527782	
3628901223	- 3629002223	
LIST 10		
Ernest Boas	- Ernest Boas	1 2 3 4 5
Rankin Barne	- Rankin Barnes	
Edward Appley	- Edward Appely	
Camel	- Camel	
Caiger Food Co.	- Caiger Food Co.	
LIST 11		
6273	- 6273	1 2 3 4 5
322	- 332	
15672839	- 15672839	
63728192637	- 63728192639	
738	- 738	
LIST 12		
Wells Fargo Co.	- Wells Fargo Co.	1 2 3 4 5
W.D. Brett	- W.D. Britt	
Tassco Co.	- Tassko Co.	
Republic Mills	- Republic Mill	
R.W. Burnham	- R.W. Burhnam	

		CIRCLE CORRECT ANSWER
LIST 13		
7253529152	- 7283529152	1 2 3 4 5
6283	- 6383	
52839102738	- 5283910238	
308	- 398	
82637201927	- 8263720127	
LIST 14		
Schumacker Co.	- Shumacker Co.	1 2 3 4 5
C.H. Caiger	- C.H. Caiger	
Abraham Strauss	- Abram Straus	
B.F. Boettjer	- B.F. Boettijer	
Cut-Rate Store	- Cut-Rate Stores	
LIST 15		
15273826	- 15273826	1 2 3 4 5
72537	- 73537	
726391027384	- 72639107384	
637389	- 627399	
725382910	- 725382910	
LIST 16		
Hixby Ltd.	- Hixby Lt'd.	1 2 3 4 5
S. Reiner	- S. Riener	
Reynard Co.	- Reynord Co.	
Esso Gassoline Co.	- Esso Gasolene Co.	
Belle Brock	- Belle Brock	
LIST 17		
7245	- 7245	1 2 3 4 5
819263728192	- 819263728172	
682537289	- 682537298	
789	- 789	
82936542891	- 82936542891	
LIST 18		
Joseph Cartwright	- Joseph Cartwrite	1 2 3 4 5
Foote Food Co.	- Foot Food Co.	
Weiman & Held	- Weiman & Held	
Sanderson Shoe Co.	- Sandersen Shoe Co.	
A.M. Byrne	- A.N. Byrne	
LIST 19		
4738267	- 4738277	1 2 3 4 5
63728	- 63729	
6283628901	- 6283628991	
918264	- 918264	
263728192037	- 2637728192073	

		CIRCLE CORRECT ANSWER
LIST 20		
Exray Laboratories	- Exray Labratories	1 2 3 4 5
Curley Toy Co.	- Curly Toy Co.	
J. Lauer & Cross	- J. Laeur & Cross	
Mireco Brands	- Mireco Brands	
Sandor Lorand	- Sandor Larand	
LIST 21		
607	- 609	1 2 3 4 5
6405	- 6403	
976	- 996	
101267	- 101267	
2065432	- 20965432	
LIST 22		
John Macy & Sons	- John Macy & Son	1 2 3 4 5
Venus Pencil Co.	- Venus Pencil Co,	
Nell McGinnis	- Nell McGinnis	
McCutcheon & Co.	- McCutcheon & Co.	
Sun-Tan Oil	- Sun-Tan Oil	
LIST 23		
703345700	- 703345700	1 2 3 4 5
46754	- 466754	
3367490	- 3367490	
3379	- 3778	
47384	- 47394	
LIST 24		
arthritis	- athritis	1 2 3 4 5
asthma	- asthma	
endocrene	- endocrene	
gastro-enterological	- gastrol-enteralogical	
orthopedic	- orthopedic	
LIST 25		
743829432	- 743828432	1 2 3 4 5
998	- 998	
732816253902	- 732816252902	
46829	- 46830	
7439120249	- 7439210249	

KEY (CORRECT ANSWERS)

1. 4
2. 3
3. 2
4. 1
5. 2
6. 1
7. 2
8. 1
9. 1
10. 3
11. 3
12. 1
13. 1
14. 1
15. 2
16. 1
17. 3
18. 1
19. 1
20. 1
21. 1
22. 4
23. 2
24. 3
25. 1

NAME AND NUMBER CHECKING
EXAMINATION SECTION
TEST 1

DIRECTIONS: Each question or incomplete statement is followed by several suggested answers or completions. Select the one that *BEST* answers the question or completes the statement. *PRINT THE LETTER OF THE CORRECT ANSWER IN THE SPACE AT THE RIGHT.*

Questions 1-10

DIRECTIONS: Questions 1 through 10 below present the identification numbers, initials, and last names of employees enrolled in a city retirement system. You are to choose the option (A, B, C, or D) that has the *identical* identification number, initials, and last name as those given in each question.

SAMPLE QUESTION

B145698 JL Jones

A. B146798 JL Jones
B. B145698 JL Jonas
C. P145698 JL Jones
D. B145698 JL Jones

The correct answer is D. Only option D shows the identification number, initials and last name exactly as they are in the sample question. Options A, B, and C have errors in the identification number or last name.

1. J297483 PL Robinson 1.____

A. J294783 PL Robinson
B. J297483 PL Robinson
C. J297483 PI Robinson
D. J297843 PL Robinson

2. S497662 JG Schwartz 2.____

A. S497662 JG Schwarz
B. S497762 JG Schwartz
C. S497662 JG Schwartz
D. S497663 JG Schwartz

3. G696436 LN Alberton 3.____

A. G696436 LM Alberton
B. G696436 LN Albertson
C. G696346 LN Albertson
D. G696436 LN Alberton

4. R774923 AD Aldrich 4.____

A. R774923 AD Aldrich
B. R744923 AD Aldrich
C. R774932 AP Aldrich
D. R774932 AD Allrich

5. N239638 RP Hrynyk 5.____

A. N236938 PR Hrynyk
B. N236938 RP Hrynyk
C. N239638 PR Hrynyk
D. N239638 RP Hrynyk

6. R156949 LT Carlson 6.____

A. R156949 LT Carlton
B. R156494 LT Carlson
C. R159649 LT Carlton
D. R156949 LT Carlson

7. T524697 MN Orenstein 7.____

A. T524697 MN Orenstein
B. T524967 MN Orinstein
C. T524697 NM Ornstein
D. T524967 NM Orenstein

8. L346239 JD Remsen 8.____

A. L346239 JD Remson
B. L364239 JD Remsen
C. L346329 JD Remsen
D. L346239 JD Remsen

9. P966438 SB Rieperson 9.____

A. P996438 SB Reiperson
B. P966438 SB Reiperson
C. R996438 SB Rieperson
D. P966438 SB Rieperson

10. D749382 CD Thompson 10.____

A. P749382 CD Thompson
B. D749832 CD Thomsonn
C. D749382 CD Thompson
D. D749823 CD Thomspon

Questions 11 - 20

DIRECTIONS: Each of Questions 11 through 20 gives the identification number and name of a person who has received treatment at a certain hospital. You are to choose the option (A, B, C, or D) which has *EXACTLY* the same identification number and name as those given in the question.

SAMPLE QUESTION

123765 Frank Y. Jones

A. 123675 Frank Y. Jones
B. 123765 Frank T. Jones
C. 123765 Frank Y. Johns
D. 123765 Frank Y. Jones

The correct answer is D. Only option D shows the identification number and name exactly as they are in the sample question. Option A has a mistake in the identification number. Option B has a mistake in the middle initial of the name. Option C has a mistake in the last name.

Now answer Questions 11 through 20 in the same manner.

11. 754898 Diane Malloy 11.____

A. 745898 Diane Malloy
B. 754898 Dion Malloy
C. 754898 Diane Malloy
D. 754898 Diane Maloy

12. 661818 Ferdinand Figueroa 12.____

A. 661818 Ferdinand Figeuroa
B. 661618 Ferdinand Figueroa
C. 661818 Ferdnand Figueroa
D. 661818 Ferdinand Figueroa

13. 100101 Norman D. Braustein 13.____

A. 100101 Norman D. Braustein
B. 101001 Norman D. Braustein
C. 100101 Norman P. Braustien
D. 100101 Norman D. Bruastein

14. 838696 Robert Kittredge
A. 838969 Robert Kittredge
B. 838696 Robert Kittredge
C. 388696 Robert Kittredge
D. 838696 Robert Kittridge
14.____

15. 243716 Abraham Soletsky
A. 243716 Abrahm Soletsky
B. 243716 Abraham Solestky
C. 243176 Abraham Soletsky
D. 243716 Abraham Soletsky
15.____

16. 981121 Phillip M. Maas
A. 981121 Phillip M. Mass
B. 981211 Phillip M. Maas
C. 981121 Phillip M. Maas
D. 981121 Phillip N. Maas
16.____

17. 786556 George Macalusso
A. 785656 George Macalusso
B. 786556 George Macalusso
C. 786556 George Maculasso
D. 786556 George Macluasso
17.____

18. 639472 Eugene Weber
A. 639472 Eugene Weber
B. 639472 Eugene Webre
C. 693472 Eugene Weber
D. 639742 Eugene Weber
18.____

19. 724936 John J. Lomonaco
A. 724936 John J. Lomanoco
B. 724396 John J. Lomonaco
C. 724936 John J. Lomonaco
D. 724936 John J. Lamonaco
19.____

20. 899868 Michael Schnitzer
A. 899868 Micheal Schnitzer
B. 898968 Michael Schnizter
C. 899688 Michael Schnitzer
D. 899868 Michael Schnitzer
20.____

Questions: 21 - 28

DIRECTIONS: Questions 21 through 28 consist of lines of names, dates, and numbers which represent the names. membership dates, social security numbers, and members of the retirement system.For each question you are to choose the option (A, B, C, or D) in Column II which *EXACTLY* matches the information in Column I.

SAMPLE QUESTION

Column I	Column II
Crossen 12/23/56 173568929 253492	A. Crossen 2/23/56 173568929 253492
	B. Crossen 12/23/56 173568729 253492
	C. Crossen 12/23/56 173568929 253492
	D. Crossan 12/23/56 173568929 258492

The correct answer is C. Only option C shows the name, date, and numbers exactly as they are in Column I. Option A has a mistake in the date. Option B has a mistake in the social security number. Option D has a mistake in the name and in the membership number.

21. Figueroa 1/15/64 119295386 147563 21.____

A. Figueroa 1/5/64 119295386 147563
B. Figueroa 1/15/64 119295386 147563
C. Figueroa 1/15/64 119295836 147563
D. Figueroa 1/15/64 119295886 147563

22. Goodridge 6/19/59 106237869 128352 22.____

A. Goodridge 6/19/59 106287869 128332
B. Goodrigde 6/19/59 106237869 128352
C. Goodridge 6/9/59 106237869 128352
D. Goodridge 6/19/59 106237869 128352

23. Balsam 9/13/57 109652382 116938 23.____

A. Balsan 9/13/57 109652382 116938
B. Balsam 9/13/57 109652382 116938
C. Balsom 9/13/57 109652382 116938
D. Balsalm 9/13/57 109652382 116938

24. Mackenzie 2/16/49 127362513 101917 24.____

A. Makenzie 2/16/49 127362513 101917
B. Mackenzie 2/16/49 127362513 101917
C. Mackenzie 2/16/49 127362513 101977
D. Mackenzie 2/16/49 127862513 101917

25. Halpern 12/2/73 115206359 286070 25.____

A. Halpern 12/2/73 115206359 286070
B. Halpern 12/2/73 113206359 286070
C. Halpern 12/2/73 115206359 206870
D. Halpern 12/2/73 115206359 286870

26. Phillips 4/8/66 137125516 192612 26.____

A. Phillips 4/8/66 137125516 196212
B. Philipps 4/8/66 137125516 192612
C. Phillips 4/8/66 137125516 192612
D. Phillips 4/8/66 137122516 192612

27. Francisce 11/9/63 123926037 152210 27.____

A. Francisce 11/9/63 123826837 152210
B. Francisce 11/9/63 123926037 152210
C. Francisce 11/9/63 123936037 152210
D. Franscice 11/9/63 123926037 152210

28. Silbert 7/28/54 118421999 178514 28.____

A.	Silbert	7/28/54	118421999	178544
B.	Silbert	7/28/54	184421999	178514
C.	Silbert	7/28/54	118421999	178514
D.	Siblert	7/28/54	118421999	178514

KEY (CORRECT ANSWERS)

1. B
2. C
3. D
4. A
5. D
6. D
7. A
8. D
9. D
10. C
11. C
12. D
13. A
14. B
15. D
16. C
17. B
18. A
19. C
20. D
21. B
22. D
23. B
24. B
25. A
26. C
27. B
28. C

TEST 2

Questions 1-3

DIRECTIONS: Items 1 to 3 are a test of your proofreading ability. Each item consists of Copy I and Copy II. You are to assume that Copy I in each item is correct. Copy II, which is meant to be a duplicate of Copy I, may contain some typographical errors. In each item, compare Copy II with Copy I and determine the number of errors in Copy II. If there are:

no errors, mark your answer A;
1 or 2 errors, mark your answer B;
3 or 4 errors, mark your answer C;
5 or 6 errors, mark your answer D;
7 errors or more, mark your answer E.

1. 1._____

COPY I

The Commissioner, before issuing any such license, shall cause an investigation to be made of the premises named and described in such application, to determine whether all the provisions of the sanitary code, building code, state industrial code, state minimum wage law, local laws, regulations of municipal agencies, and other requirements of this article are fully observed. (Section B32-169.0 of Article 23.)

COPY II

The Commissioner, before issuing any such license shall cause an investigation to be made of the premises named and described in such applecation, to determine whether all the provisions of the sanitary code, bilding code, state industrial code, state minimum wage laws, local laws, regulations of municipal agencies, and other requirements of this article are fully observed. (Section E32-169.0 of Article 23.)

2. 2._____

COPY I

Among the persons who have been appointed to various agencies are John Queen, 9 West 55th Street, Brooklyn; Joseph Blount, 2497 Durward Road, Bronx: Lawrence K. Eberhardt, 3194 Bedford Street, Manhattan; Reginald L. Darcy, 1476 Allerton Drive, Bronx; and Benjamin Ledwith, 177 Greene Street, Manhattan.

COPY II

Among the persons who have been appointed to various agencies are John Queen, 9 West 56th Street, Brooklyn, Joseph Blount, 2497 Dureward Road, Bronx: Lawrence K. Eberhart , 3194 Belford Street, Manhattan; Reginald L. Barcey, 1476 Allerton drive, Bronx; and Benjamin Ledwith, 177 Green Street, Manhattan.

3. 3._____

COPY I

Except as hereinafter provided, it shall be unlawful to use, store or have on hand any inflammable motion picture film in quantities greater than one standard or two sub-standard reels, or aggregating more than two thousand feet in length, or more than ten pounds in weight without the permit required by this section.

COPY II

Except as herinafter provided, it shall be unlawfull to use, store or have on hand any inflamable motion picture film, in quantities greater than one standard or two substandard reels or aggregating more than two thousand feet in length, or more then ten pounds in weight without the permit required by this section.

Questions 4-6

Questions 4 to 6 are a test of your proofreading ability. Each question consists of Copy I and Copy II. You are to assume that Copy I in each question is correct. Copy II, which is meant to be a duplicate of Copy I, may contain some typographical errors. In each question, compare Copy II with Copy I and determine the number of errors in Copy II. If there are

no errors, mark your answer A;
1 or 2 errors, mark your answer B;
3 or 4 errors, mark your answer C;
5 errors or more, mark your answer D.

4. 4.____

COPY I

It shall be unlawful to install wires or appliances for electric light, heat or power, operating at a potential in excess of seven hundred fifty volts, in or on any part of a building, with the exception of a central station, sub-station, transformer, or switching vault, or motor room; provided, however, that the Commissioner may authorize the use of radio transmitting apparatus under special conditions.

COPY II

It shall be unlawful to install wires or appliances for electric light, heat or power, operating at a potential in excess of seven hundred fifty volts, in or on any part of a building, with the exception of a central station, sub-station, transformer, or switching vault, or motor room, provided, however, that the Commissioner may authorize the use of radio transmitting apperatus under special conditions.

5. 5.____

COPY I

The grand total debt service for the fiscal year 2006-07 amounts to $350,563,718.63, as compared with $309,561,347.27 for the current fiscal year, or an increase of $41,002,371.36. The amount payable from other sources in 2006-07 shows an increase of $13,264,165.47, resulting in an increase of $27,733,205.89 payable from tax levy funds.

COPY II

The grand total debt service for the fiscal year 2006-07 amounts to $350,568,718.63, as compared with $309,561,347.27 for the current fiscel year, or an increase of $41,002,371.36. The amount payable from other sources in 2006-07 show an increase of $13,264,165.47 resulting in an increase of $27,733,295.89 payable from tax levy funds.

6. 6.____

COPY I

The following site proposed for the new building is approximately rectangular in shape and comprises an entire block, having frontages of about 721 feet on 16th Road, 200 feet on 157th Street, 721 feet on 17th Avenue and 200 feet on 154th Street, with a gross area of about 144,350 square feet. The 2006-07 assessed valuation is $28,700,000 of which $6,000,000 is for improvements.

COPY II

The following site proposed for the new building is approximately rectangular in shape and comprises an entire block, having frontage of about 721 feet on 16th Road, 200 feet on 157th Street, 721 feet on 17th Avenue, and 200 feet on 134th Street, with a gross area of about 114,350 square feet. The 2006-07 assessed valuation is $28,700,000 of which $6,000,000 is for improvements.

KEY (CORRECT ANSWERS)

1. D
2. E
3. E
4. B
5. D
6. C

TEST 3

Questions 1-8

DIRECTIONS: Each of the Questions numbered 1 through 8 consists of three sets of names and name codes. In each question, the two names and name codes on the same line are supposed to be exactly the same.

Look carefully at each set of names and codes and mark your answer

A. if there are mistakes in all three sets
B. if there are mistakes in two of the sets
C. if there is a mistake in only one set
D. if there are no mistakes in any of the sets

<u>SAMPLE QUESTION</u>

The following sample question is given to help you understand the procedure

Macabe, John N. - V 53162	Macade, John N. - V 53162
Howard, Joan S. - J 24791	Howard, Joan S. - J 24791
Ware, Susan B. - A 45068	Ware, Susan B. - A 45968

In the above sample question, the names and name codes of the first set are not exactly the same because of the spelling of the last name (Macabe - Macade). The names and name codes of the second set are exactly the same. The names and name codes of the third set are not exactly the same because the two name codes are different (A 45068 - A 45968). Since there are mistakes in only 2 of the sets,the answer to the sample question is B.

1.	Powell, Michael C. - 78537 F Martinez, Pablo J. - 24435 P MacBane, Eliot M. - 98674 E	Powell, Michael C. - 78537 F Martinez, Pablo J. - 24435 P MacBane, Eliot M. - 98674 E	1._____
2.	Fitz-Kramer Machines Inc. - 259090 Marvel Cleaning Service - 482657 Donato, Carl G. - 637418	Fitz-Kramer Machines Inc. - 259090 Marvel Cleaning Service - 482657 Danato, Carl G. - 687418	2._____
3.	Martin Davison Trading Corp. - 43108 T Cotwald Lighting Fixtures - 76065 L R. Crawford Plumbers - 23157 C	Martin Davidson Trading Corp. - 43108 T Cotwald Lighting Fixtures - 70056 L R. Crawford Plumbers - 23157 G	3._____

	Column I	Column II	
4.	Fraiman Engineering Corp. - M4773 Neuman, Walter B. - N7745 Pierce, Eric M. - W6304	Friaman Engineering Corp. - M4773 Neumen, Walter B. - N7745 Pierce, Eric M. - W6304	4.____
5.	Constable, Eugene - B 64837 Derrick, Paul - H 27119 Heller, Karen - S 49606	Comstable, Eugene - B 64837 Derrik, Paul - H 27119 Heller, Karen - S 46906	5.____
6.	Hernando Delivery Service Co. - D 7456 Barettz Electrical Supplies - N 5392 Tanner, Abraham - M 4798	Hernando Delivery Service Co. - D 7456 Barettz Electrical Supplies - N 5392 Tanner, Abraham - M 4798	6.____
7.	Kalin Associates - R 38641 Sealey, Robert E. - P 63533 Seals! Office Furniture - R36742	Kaline Associates - R 38641 Sealey, Robert E. - P 63553 Seals! Office Furniture - R36742	7.____
8.	Janowsky, Philip M.- 742213 Hansen, Thomas H. - 934816 L. Lester and Son Inc. - 294568	Janowsky, Philip M.- 742213 Hanson, Thomas H. - 934816 L. Lester and Son Inc. - 294568	8.____

Questions 9-13

DIRECTIONS: Each of the questions number 9 through 13 consists of three sets of names and building codes. In each question, the two names and building codes on the same line are supposed to be exactly the same.

If you find an error or errors on only *one* of the sets in the question, mark your answer A; any *two* of the sets in the question, mark your answer B; all *three* of the sets in the question, mark your answer C; *none* of the sets in the question, mark your answer D.

Column I	Column II
Duvivier, Anne P. - X52714	Duviver, Anne P. - X52714
Dyrborg, Alfred - B4217	Dyrborg, Alfred - B4267
Dymnick, JoAnne - P482596	Dymnick, JoAnne - P482596

In the above sample question, the first set of names and building codes is not exactly the same because the last names are spelled differently (Duvivier - Duviver). The second set of names and building codes is not exactly the same because the building codes are different (B4217 - B4267). The third set of names and building codes is exactly the same. Since there are mistakes in two of the sets of names and building codes, the answer to the sample question is B.

Now answer the questions on the following page using, the same procedure.

	Column I	Column II	
9.	Lautmann, Gerald G. - C2483 Lawlor, Michael - W44639 Lawrence, John J. - H1358	Lautmann, Gerald C. - C2483 Lawler, Michael - W44639 Lawrence, John J. - H1358	9.____
10.	Mittmann, Howard - J4113 Mitchell, William T.- M75271 Milan, T. Thomas - Q67533	Mittmann, Howard - J4113 Mitchell, William T.- M75271 Milan, T. Thomas - Q67553	10.____
11.	Quarles, Vincent - J34760 Quinn, Alan N. - S38813 Quinones, Peter W. - B87467	Quarles, Vincent - J34760 Quinn, Alan N. - S38813 Quinones, Peter W. - B87467	11.____
12.	Daniels, Harold H. - A26554 Dantzler, Richard - C35780 Davidson, Martina - E62901	Daniels, Harold H - A26544 Dantzler, Richard - 035780 Davidson, Martin - E62901	12.____
13.	Graham, Cecil J. - I20244 Granger, Deborah - T86211 Grant, Charles L. - G5788	Graham, Cecil J. - I20244 Granger, Deborah - T86211 Grant, Charles L. - G5788	13.____

KEY (CORRECT ANSWERS)

1.	D	8.	C
2.	C	9.	B
3.	A	10.	A
4.	B	11.	D
5.	A	12.	C
6.	D	13.	D
7.	B		

TEST 4

Questions 1-9

DIRECTIONS: In questions 1 to 10 there are five pairs of numbers or letters and numbers. Compare each pair and decide how many pairs are *EXACTLY ALIKE. PRINT THE LETTER OF THE CORRECT ANSWER IN THE SPACE AT THE RIGHT.*

A. if only one pair is exactly alike
B. if only two pairs are exactly alike
C. if only three pairs are exactly alike
D. if only four pairs are exactly alike
E. if all five pairs are exactly alike

1. 73-F......F-73 FF-73. . . .FF-73 1.____
F-7373....F-7373 373-FF...337-FF
F-733.....337-F

2. 0-17158. . ..0-17158 0-71518 ... 0-71518 2.____
0-11758....0-11758 0-15817... 0-15817
0-51178....0-51178

3. 1A-7908....1A-7908 7A-8901....7A-8091 3.____
7A-891.....7A-891 1A-9078....1A-9708.
9A-7018....9A-7081

4. 2V-6426....2V-6246 2N-6246....2N-6246 4.____
2V-6426....2N-6426 2N-6624....2N-6624
2V-6462....2V-6462

5. 3NY-56......3ny-65 5NY-356.....3NY-356 5.____
6NY-3566....3ny-3566 5NY-6536....5NY-6536
3NY-5663....5ny-3663

6. COB-065....COB-065 BCL-506....BCL-506 6.____
LBC-650....LBC-650 DLB-560....DLB-560
CDB-056....COB-065

7. 4KQ-9130....4KQ-9130 4KQ-9310....4KQ-9130 7.____
4KQ-9031....4KQ-9031 4KQ-9301....4KQ-9301
4KQ-9013....4KQ-9013

8. MK-89......MK-98 98-MK......89-MK 8.____
MSK-998........MSK-998 MOSK.......MOKS
SMK-899....SMK-899

9. 8MD-2104....SMD-2014 2MD-8140....2MD-8140 9.____
814-MD......814-MD 4MD-8201. . . .4MD-8201
MD-281......MD-481

10. 161-035. .. .161-035 150-316.... 150-316 10.____
315-160....315-160 131-650....131-650
165-301....165-301

KEY (CORRECT ANSWERS)

1. B
2. E
3. B
4. C
5. A
6. D
7. D
8. B
9. C
10. E

TEST 5

DIRECTIONS: Each question or incomplete statement is followed by several suggested answers or completions. Select the one that *BEST* answers the question or completes the statement. *PRINT THE LETTER OF THE CORRECT ANSWER IN THE SPACE AT THE RIGHT.*

Questions 1-5

DIRECTIONS: Questions 1 through 5, inclusive, consist of groups of four displays representing license identification plates. Examine each group of plates and determine the number of plates in each group which are identical. Mark your answer sheets as follows:

If only two plates are identical, mark answer A.
If only three plates are identical, mark answer B.
If all four plates are identical, mark answer C.
If the plates are all different, mark answer D

<u>*EXAMPLE*</u>

ABC123 BCD123 ABC123 BCD235

Since only two plates are identical, the first and the third, the correct answer is A.

1.	PBV839	PVB839	PVB839	PVB839	1.____
2.	WTX083	WTX083	WTX083	WTX083	2.____
3.	B73609	D73906	BD7396	BD7906	3.____
4.	AK7423	AK7423	AK1423	A81324	4.____
5.	583Y10	683Y10	583Y01	583Y10	5.____

Questions 6-10

DIRECTIONS: Questions 6 through 10 consist of groups of numbers and letters similar to those which might appear on license plates. Each group of numbers and letters will be called a license identification. Choose the license identification lettered A, B, C, or D that *EXACTLY* matches the license identification shown next to the question number.

SAMPLE
NY 1977
ABC-123

A. NY 1976 ABC-123 B. NY 1977 ABC-132 C. NY 1977 CBA-123 D. NY 1977 ABC-123

The license identification given is NY 1977. The only choice ABC-123. that exactly matches it is the license identification next to the letter D. The correct answer is therefore D.

6. NY 1976 QLT-781 6.____

A. NJ 1976 QLT-781 B. NY 1975 QLT-781 C. NY 1976 QLT-781 D. NY 1977 QLT-781

7. FLA 1977 2-7LT58J 7.____

A. FLA 1977 2-7TL58J B. FLA 1977 2-7LTJ58 C. FLA 1977 2-7LT58J D. LA 1977 2-7LT58J

8. NY 1975 OQC383 8.____

A. NY 1975 OQC383 B. NY 1975 OQC833 C. NY 1975 QCQ383 D. NY 1977 OCQ383

9. MASS 1977 B-8DK02 9.____

A. MISS 1977 B-8DK02 B. MASS 1977 B-8DK02 C. MASS 1976 B-8DK02 D. MASS 1977 B-80KD2

10. NY 1976 ZV0586 10.____

A. NY 1976 2V0586 B. NY 1977 ZV0586 C. NY 1976 ZV0586 D. NY 1976 ZU0586

KEY (CORRECT ANSWERS)

1. B	6. C
2. C	7. C
3. D	8. A
4. A	9. B
5. A	10. C

TEST 6

DIRECTIONS: Assume that each of the capital letters in the table below represents the name of an employee enrolled in the city employees' retirement system. The number directly beneath the letter represents the agency for which the employee works, and the small letter directly beneath represents the code for the employee's account.

Name of Employee	L	O	T	Q	A	M	R	N	C
Agency	3	4	5	9	8	7	2	1	6
Account Code	r	f	b	i	d	t	g	e	n

In each of the following questions 1 through 3, the agency code numbers and the account code letters in Columns 2 and 3 should correspond to the capital letters in Column 1 and should be in the same consecutive order. For each question, look at each column carefully and mark your answer as follows:
If there are one or more errors *in Column 2 only* , mark your answer A.
If there are one or more errors *in Column 3 only,* mark your answer B.
If there are one or more errors in Column 2 and one or more errors in Column 3, mark your answer C.
If there are *NO* errors in either column, mark your answer D.
The following sample question is given to help you understand the procedure.

Column I	Column 2	Column 3
TQLMOC	583746	birtfn

In Column 2, the second agency code number (corresponding to letter Q) should be "9", not "8". Column 3 is coded correctly to Column 1. Since there is an error only in Column 2, the correct answer is A.

	Column 1	Column 2	Column 3	
1.	Q L N R C A	9 3 1 2 6 8	i r e g n d	1.____
2.	N R M O T C	1 2 7 5 4 6	e g f t b n	2.____
3.	R C T A L M	2 6 5 8 3 7	g n d b r t	3.____

KEY (CORRECT ANSWERS)

1. D
2. C
3. B

EXAMINATION SECTION
TEST 1

DIRECTIONS: In each of the following questions, only one of the four sentences conforms to standards of correct usage. The other three contain errors in grammar, diction, or punctuation. Select the choice in each question which BEST conforms to standards of correct usage. Consider a choice correct if it contains none of the errors mentioned above, even though there may be other ways of expressing the same thought. *PRINT THE LETTER OF THE CORRECT ANSWER IN THE SPACE AT THE RIGHT.*

1. A. Because he was ill was no excuse for his behavior. 1.____
   B. I insist that he see a lawyer before he goes to trial.
   C. He said "that he had not intended to go."
   D. He wasn't out of the office only three days.

2. A. He came to the station and pays a porter to carry his bags into the train. 2.____
   B. I should have liked to live in medieval times.
   C. My father was born in Linville. A little country town where everyone knows everyone else.
   D. The car, which is parked across the street, is disabled.

3. A. He asked the desk clerk for a clean, quiet, room. 3.____
   B. I expected James to be lonesome and that he would want to go home.
   C. I have stopped worrying because I have heard nothing further on the subject.
   D. If the board of directors controls the company, they may take actions which are disapproved by the stockholders.

4. A. Each of the players knew their place. 4.____
   B. He whom you saw on the stage is the son of an actor.
   C. Susan is the smartest of the twin sisters.
   D. Who ever thought of him winning both prizes?

5. A. An outstanding trait of early man was their reliance on omens. 5.____
   B. Because I had never been there before.
   C. Neither Mr. Jones nor Mr. Smith has completed his work.
   D. While eating my dinner, a dog came to the window.

6. A. A copy of the lease, in addition to the Rules and Regulations, are to be given to each tenant. 6.____
   B. The Rules and Regulations and a copy of the lease is being given to each tenant.
   C. A copy of the lease, in addition to the Rules and Regulations, is to be given to each tenant.
   D. A copy of the lease, in addition to the Rules and Regulations, are being given to each tenant.

7. A. Although we understood that for him music was a passion, we were disturbed by the fact that he was addicted to sing along with the soloists. 7.____
   B. Do you believe that Steven is liable to win a scholarship?
   C. Give the picture to whomever is a connoisseur of art.
   D. Whom do you believe to be the most efficient worker in the office?

8. A. Each adult who is sure they know all the answers will some day realize their mistake. 8.____
   B. Even the most hardhearted villain would have to feel bad about so horrible a tragedy.
   C. Neither being licensed teachers, both aspirants had to pass rigorous tests before being appointed.
   D. The principal reason why he wanted to be designated was because he had never before been to a convention.

9. A. Being that the weather was so inclement, the party has been postponed for at least a month. 9.____
   B. He is in New York City only three weeks and he has already seen all the thrilling sights in Manhattan and in the other four boroughs.
   C. If you will look it up in the official directory, which can be consulted in the library during specified hours, you will discover that the chairman and director are Mr. T. Henry Long.
   D. Working hard at college during the day and at the post office during the night, he appeared to his family to be indefatigable.

10. A. I would have been happy to oblige you if you only asked me to do it. 10.____
    B. The cold weather, as well as the unceasing wind and rain, have made us decide to spend the winter in Florida.
    C. The politician would have been more successful in winning office if he would have been less dogmatic.
    D. These trousers are expensive; however, they will wear well.

11. A. All except him wore formal attire at the reception for the ambassador. 11.____
    B. If that chair were to be blown off of the balcony, it might injure someone below.
    C. Not a passenger, who was in the crash, survived the impact.
    D. To borrow money off friends is the best way to lose them.

12. A. Approaching Manhattan on the ferry boat from Staten Island, an unforgettable sight of the skyscrapers is seen. 12.____
    B. Did you see the exhibit of modernistic paintings as yet?
    C. Gesticulating wildly and ranting in stentorian tones, the speaker was the sinecure of all eyes.
    D. The airplane with crew and passengers was lost somewhere in the Pacific Ocean.

13. A. If one has consistently had that kind of training, it is certainly too late to change your entire method of swimming long distances. 13.____
    B. The captain would have been more impressed if you would have been more conscientious in evacuation drills.
    C. The passengers on the stricken ship were all ready to abandon it at the signal.
    D. The villainous shark lashed at the lifeboat with it's tail, trying to upset the rocking boat in order to partake of it's contents.

14. A. As one whose been certified as a professional engineer, I believe that the decision to build a bridge over that harbor is unsound. 14._____
    B. Between you and me, this project ought to be completed long before winter arrives.
    C. He fervently hoped that the men would be back at camp and to find them busy at their usual chores.
    D. Much to his surprise, he discovered that the climate of Korea was like his home town.

15. A. An industrious executive is aided, not impeded, by having a hobby which gives him a fresh point of view on life and its problems. 15._____
    B. Frequent absence during the calendar year will surely mitigate against the chances of promotion.
    C. He was unable to go to the committee meeting because he was very ill.
    D. Mr. Brown expressed his disapproval so emphatically that his associates were embarassed.

16. A. At our next session, the office manager will have told you something about his duties and responsibilities. 16._____
    B. In general, the book is absorbing and original and have no hesitation about recommending it.
    C. The procedures followed by private industry in dealing with lateness and absence are different from ours.
    D. We shall treat confidentially any information about Mr. Doe, to whom we understand you have sent reports to for many years.

17. A. I talked to one official, whom I knew was fully impartial. 17._____
    B. Everyone signed the petition but him.
    C. He proved not only to be a good student but also a good athlete.
    D. All are incorrect.

18. A. Every year a large amount of tenants are admitted to housing projects. 18._____
    B. Henry Ford owned around a billion dollars in industrial equipment.
    C. He was aggravated by the child's poor behavior.
    D. All are incorrect.

19. A. Before he was committed to the asylum he suffered from the illusion that he was Napoleon. 19._____
    B. Besides stocks, there were also bonds in the safe.
    C. We bet the other team easily.
    D. All are incorrect.

20. A. Bring this report to your supervisor immediately. 20._____
    B. He set the chair down near the table.
    C. The capitol of New York is Albany.
    D. All are incorrect.

21. A. He was chosen to arbitrate the dispute because everyone knew he would be disinterested. 21._____
    B. It is advisable to obtain the best council before making an important decision.
    C. Less college students are interested in teaching than ever before.
    D. All are incorrect.

22. A. She, hearing a signal, the source lamp flashed. 22.____
    B. While hearing a signal, the source lamp flashed.
    C. In hearing a signal, the source lamp flashed.
    D. As she heard a signal, the source lamp flashed.

23. A. Every one of the time records have been initialed in the designated spaces. 23.____
    B. All of the time records has been initialed in the designated spaces.
    C. Each one of the time records was initialed in the designated spaces.
    D. The time records all been initialed in the designated spaces.

24. A. If there is no one else to answer the phone, you will have to answer it. 24.____
    B. You will have to answer it yourself if no one else answers the phone.
    C. If no one else is not around to pick up the phone, you will have to do it.
    D. You will have to answer the phone when nobodys here to do it.

25. A. Dr. Barnes not in his office. What could I do for you? 25.____
    B. Dr. Barnes is not in his office. Is there something I can do for you?
    C. Since Dr. Barnes is not in his office, might there be something I may do for you?
    D. Is there any ways I can assist you since Dr. Barnes is not in his office?

26. A. She do not understand how the new console works. 26.____
    B. The way the new console works, she doesn't understand.
    C. She doesn't understand how the new console works.
    D. The new console works, so that she doesn't understand.

27. A. Certain changes in family income must be reported as they occur. 27.____
    B. When certain changes in family income occur, it must be reported.
    C. Certain family income changes must be reported as they occur.
    D. Certain changes in family income must be reported as they have been occuring.

28. A. Each tenant has to complete the application themselves. 28.____
    B. Each of the tenants have to complete the application by himself.
    C. Each of the tenants has to complete the application himself.
    D. Each of the tenants has to complete the application by themselves.

29. A. Yours is the only building that the construction will effect. 29.____
    B. Your's is the only building affected by the construction.
    C. The construction will only effect your building.
    D. Yours is the only building that will be affected by the construction.

30. A. There is four tests left. 30.____
    B. The number of tests left are four.
    C. There are four tests left.
    D. Four of the tests remains.

31. A. Each of the applicants takes a test. 31.____
    B. Each of the applicants take a test.
    C. Each of the applicants take tests.
    D. Each of the applicants have taken tests.

32. A. The applicant, not the examiners, are ready. 32.____
    B. The applicants, not the examiner, is ready.
    C. The applicants, not the examiner, are ready.
    D. The applicant, not the examiner, are ready.

33. A. You will not progress except you practice. 33.____
    B. You will not progress without you practicing.
    C. You will not progress unless you practice.
    D. You will not progress provided you do not practice.

34. A. Neither the director or the employees will be at the office tomorrow. 34.____
    B. Neither the director nor the employees will be at the office tomorrow.
    C. Neither the director, or the secretary nor the other employees will be at the office tomorrow.
    D. Neither the director, the secretary or the other employees will be at the office tomorrow.

35. A. In my absence he and her will have to finish the assignment. 35.____
    B. In my absence he and she will have to finish the assignment.
    C. In my absence she and him, they will have to finish the assignment.
    D. In my absence he and her both will have to finish the assignment.

KEY (CORRECT ANSWERS)

1. B
2. B
3. C
4. B
5. C
6. C
7. D
8. B
9. D
10. D
11. A
12. D
13. C
14. B
15. A
16. C
17. B
18. D
19. B
20. B
21. A
22. D
23. C
24. A
25. B
26. C
27. A
28. C
29. D
30. C
31. A
32. C
33. C
34. B
35. B

TEST 2

DIRECTIONS: Each question or incomplete statement is followed by several suggested answers or completions. Select the one that BEST answers the question or completes the statement. *PRINT THE LETTER OF THE CORRECT ANSWER IN THE SPACE AT THE RIGHT.*

Questions 1-4.

DIRECTIONS: Questions 1 through 4 consist of three sentences each. For each question, select the sentence which contains NO error in grammar or usage.

1. A. Be sure that everybody brings his notes to the conference. 1.____
   B. He looked like he meant to hit the boy.
   C. Mr. Jones is one of the clients who was chosen to represent the district
   D. All are incorrect.

2. A. He is taller than I. 2.____
   B. I'll have nothing to do with these kind of people.
   C. The reason why he will not buy the house is because it is too expensive.
   D. All are incorrect.

3. A. Aren't I eligible for this apartment. 3.____
   B. Have you seen him anywheres?
   C. He should of come earlier.
   D. All are incorrect.

4. A. He graduated college in 1982. 4.____
   B. He hadn't but one more line to write.
   C. Who do you think is the author of this report?
   D. All are incorrect.

Questions 5-35.

DIRECTIONS: In each of the following questions, only one of the four sentences conforms to standards of correct usage. The other three contain errors in grammar, diction, or punctuation. Select the choice in each question which BEST conforms to standards of correct usage. Consider a choice correct if it contains none of the errors mentioned above, even though there may be other ways of expressing the same thought.

5. A. It is obvious that no one wants to be a kill-joy if they can help it. 5.____
   B. It is not always possible, and perhaps it never ispossible, to judge a person's character by just looking at him.
   C. When Yogi Berra of the New York Yankees hit an immortal grandslam home run, everybody in the huge stadium including Pittsburgh fans, rose to his feet.
   D. Every one of us students must pay tuition today.

6. A. The physician told the young mother that if the baby is not able to digest its milk, it should be boiled. 6._____
   B. There is no doubt whatsoever that he felt deeply hurt because John Smith had betrayed the trust.
   C. Having partaken of a most delicious repast prepared by Tessie Breen, the hostess, the horses were driven home immediately thereafter.
   D. The attorney asked my wife and myself several questions.

7. A. Despite all denials, there is no doubt in my mind that 7._____
   B. At this time everyone must deprecate the demogogic attack made by one of our Senators on one of our most revered statesmen.
   C. In the first game of a crucial two-game series, Ted Williams, got two singles, both of them driving in a run.
   D. Our visitor brought good news to John and I.

8. A. If he would have told me, I should have been glad to help him in his dire financial emergency. 8._____
   B. Newspaper men have often asserted that diplomats or so-called official spokesmen sometimes employ equivocation in attempts to deceive.
   C. I think someones coming to collect money for the Red Cross.
   D. In a masterly summation, the young attorney expressed his belief that the facts clearly militate against this opinion.

9. A. We have seen most all the exhibits. 9._____
   B. Without in the least underestimating your advice, in my opinion the situation has grown immeasurably worse in the past few days.
   C. I wrote to the box office treasurer of the hit show that a pair of orchestra seats would be preferable.
   D. As the grim story of Pearl Harbor was broadcast on that fateful December 7, it was the general opinion that war was inevitable.

10. A. Without a moment's hesitation, Casey Stengel said that Larry Berra works harder than any player on the team. 10._____
    B. There is ample evidence to indicate that many animals can run faster than any human being.
    C. No one saw the accident but I.
    D. Example of courage is the heroic defense put up by the paratroopers against overwhelming odds.

11. A. If you prefer these kind, Mrs. Grey, we shall be more than willing to let you have them reasonably. 11._____
    B. If you like these here, Mrs. Grey, we shall be more than willing to let you have them reasonably.
    C. If you like these, Mrs. Grey, we shall be more than willing to let you have them.
    D. Who shall we appoint?

12. A. The number of errors are greater in speech than in writing. 12._____
    B. The doctor rather than the nurse was to blame for his being neglected.
    C. Because the demand for these books have been so great, we reduced the price.
    D. John Galsworthy, the English novelist, could not have survived a serious illness; had it not been for loving care.

13. A. Our activities this year have seldom ever been as interesting as they have been this month. 13.____
B. Our activities this month have been more interesting, or at least as interesting as those of any month this year.
C. Our activities this month has been more interesting than those of any other month this year.
D. Neither Jean nor her sister was at home.

14. A. George B. Shaw's view of common morality, as well as his wit sparkling with a dash of perverse humor here and there, have led critics to term him "The Incurable Rebel." 14.____
B. The President's program was not always received with the wholehearted endorsement of his own party, which is why the party faces difficulty in drawing up a platform for the coming election.
C. The reason why they wanted to travel was because they had never been away from home.
D. Facing a barrage of cameras, the visiting celebrity found it extremely difficult to express his opinions clearly.

15. A. When we calmed down, we all agreed that our anger had been kind of unnecessary and had not helped the situation. 15.____
B. Without him going into all the details, he made us realize the horror of the accident.
C. Like one girl, for example, who applied for two positions.
D. Do not think that you have to be so talented as he is in order to play in the school orchestra.

16. A. He looked very peculiarly to me. 16.____
B. He certainly looked at me peculiar.
C. Due to the train's being late, we had to wait an hour.
D. The reason for the poor attendance is that it is raining.

17. A. About one out of four own an automobile. 17.____
B. The collapse of the old Mitchell Bridge was caused by defective construction in the central pier.
C. Brooks Atkinson was well acquainted with the best literature, thus helping him to become an able critic.
D. He has to stand still until the relief man comes up, thus giving him no chance to move about and keep warm.

18. A. He is sensitive to confusion and withdraws from people whom he feels are too noisy. 18.____
B. Do you know whether the data is statistically correct?
C. Neither the mayor or the aldermen are to blame.
D. Of those who were graduated from high school, a goodly percentage went to college.

19. A. Acting on orders, the offices were searched by a designated committee. 19.____
B. The answer probably is nothing.
C. I thought it to be all right to excuse them from class.
D. I think that he is as successful a singer, if not more successful, than Mary.

20. A. $120,000 is really very little to pay for such a wellbuilt house. 20.____
B. The creatures looked like they had come from outer space.
C. It was her, he knew!
D. Nobody but me knows what to do.

21. A. Mrs. Smith looked good in her new suit. 21.____
B. New York may be compared with Chicago.
C. I will not go to the meeting except you go with me.
D. I agree with this editorial.

22. A. My opinions are different from his. 22.____
B. There will be less students in class now.
C. Helen was real glad to find her watch.
D. It had been pushed off of her dresser.

23. A. Almost everone, who has been to California, returns with glowing reports. 23.____
B. George Washington, John Adams, and Thomas Jefferson, were our first presidents.
C. Mr. Walters, whom we met at the bank yesterday, is the man, who gave me my first job.
D. One should study his lessons as carefully as he can.

24. A. We had such a good time yesterday. 24.____
B. When the bell rang, the boys and girls went in the schoolhouse.
C. John had the worst headache when he got up this morning.
D. Today's assignment is somewhat longer than yesterday's.

25. A. Neither the mayor nor the city clerk are willing to talk. 25.____
B. Neither the mayor nor the city clerk is willing to talk.
C. Neither the mayor or the city clerk are willing to talk.
D. Neither the mayor or the city clerk is willing to talk.

26. A. Being that he is that kind of boy, cooperation cannot be expected. 26.____
B. He interviewed people who he thought had something to say.
C. Stop whomever enters the building regardless of rank or office held.
D. Passing through the countryside, the scenery pleased us.

27. A. The childrens' shoes were in their closet. 27.____
B. The children's shoes were in their closet.
C. The childs' shoes were in their closet.
D. The childs' shoes were in his closet.

28. A. An agreement was reached between the defendant, the plaintiff, the plaintiff's attorney and the insurance company as to the amount of the settlement. 28.____
B. Everybody was asked to give their versions of the accident.
C. The consensus of opinion was that the evidence was inconclusive.
D. The witness stated that if he was rich, he wouldn't have had to loan the money.

29. A. Before beginning the investigation, all the materials relating to the case were carefully assembled. 29.____
B. The reason for his inability to keep the appointment is because of his injury in the accident.
C. This here evidence tends to support the claim of the defendant.
D. We interviewed all the witnesses who, according to the driver, were still in town.

30. A. Each claimant was allowed the full amount of their medical expenses. 30.____
B. Either of the three witnesses is available.
C. Every one of the witnesses was asked to tell his story.
D. Neither of the witnesses are right.

31. A. The commissioner, as well as his deputy and various bureau heads, were present. 31.____
B. A new organization of employers and employees have been formed.
C. One or the other of these men have been selected.
D. The number of pages in the book is enough to discourage a reader.

32. A. Between you and me, I think he is the better man. 32.____
B. He was believed to be me.
C. Is it us that you wish to see?
D. The winners are him and her.

33. A. Beside the statement to the police, the witness spoke to no one. 33.____
B. He made no statement other than to the police and I.
C. He made no statement to any one else, aside from the police.
D. The witness spoke to no one but me.

34. A. The claimant has no one to blame but himself. 34.____
B. The boss sent us, he and I, to deliver the packages.
C. The lights come from mine and not his car.
D. There was room on the stairs for him and myself.

35. A. Admission to this clinic is limited to patients' inability to pay for medical care. 35.____
B. Patients who can pay little or nothing for medical care are treated in this clinic.
C. The patient's ability to pay for medical care is the determining factor in his admissibility to this clinic.
D. This clinic is for the patient's that cannot afford to pay or that can pay a little for medical care.

KEY (CORRECT ANSWERS)

1. A
2. A
3. D
4. C
5. D

6. D
7. B
8. B
9. D
10. B

11. C
12. B
13. D
14. D
15. D

16. D
17. B
18. D
19. B
20. D

21. A
22. A
23. D
24. D
25. B

26. B
27. B
28. C
29. D
30. C

31. D
32. A
33. D
34. A
35. B

EXAMINATION SECTION
TEST 1

DIRECTIONS: Each question or incomplete statement is followed by several suggested answers or completions. Select the one that BEST answers the question or completes the statement. *PRINT THE LETTER OF THE CORRECT ANSWER IN THE SPACE AT THE RIGHT.*

1. Which of the following sentences is punctuated INCORRECTLY? 1.____

   A. Johnson said, "One tiny virus, Blanche, can multiply so fast that it will become 200 viruses in 25 minutes."
   B. With economic pressures hitting them from all sides, American farmers have become the weak link in the food chain.
   C. The degree to which this is true, of course, depends on the personalities of the people involved, the subject matter, and the atmosphere in general.
   D. "What loneliness, asked George Eliot, is more lonely than distrust?"

2. Which of the following sentences is punctuated INCORRECTLY? 2.____

   A. Based on past experiences, do you expect the plumber to show up late, not have the right parts, and overcharge you.
   B. When polled, however, the participants were most concerned that it be convenient.
   C. No one mentioned the flavor of the coffee, and no one seemed to care that china was used instead of plastic.
   D. As we said before, sometimes people view others as things; they don't see them as living, breathing beings like themselves.

3. Convention members travelled here from Kingston New York Pittsfield Massachusetts Bennington Vermont and Hartford Connecticut. 3.____
   How many commas should there be in the above sentence?

   A. 3 B. 4 C. 5 D. 6

4. Of the two speakers the one who spoke about human rights is more famous and more humble. 4.____
   How many commas should there be in the above sentence?

   A. 1 B. 2 C. 3 D. 4

5. Which sentence is punctuated INCORRECTLY? 5.____

   A. Five people voted no; two voted yes; one person abstained.
   B. Well, consider what has been said here today, but we won't make any promises.
   C. Anthropologists divide history into three major periods: the Stone Age, the Bronze Age, and the Iron Age.
   D. Therefore, we may create a stereotype about people who are unsuccessful; we may see them as lazy, unintelligent, or afraid of success.

6. Which sentence is punctuated INCORRECTLY? 6.____

   A. Studies have found that the unpredictability of customer behavior can lead to a great deal of stress, particularly if the behavior is unpleasant or if the employee has little control over it.

B. If this degree of emotion and variation can occur in spectator sports, imagine the role that perceptions can play when there are <u>real</u> stakes involved.
C. At other times, however hidden expectations may sabotage or severely damage an encounter without anyone knowing what happened.
D. There are usually four issues to look for in a conflict: differences in values, goals, methods, and facts.

Questions 7-10.

DIRECTIONS: Questions 7 through 10 test your ability to distinguish between words that sound alike but are spelled differently and have different meanings. In the following groups of sentences, one of the underlined words is used incorrectly.

7. A. By <u>accepting</u> responsibility for their actions, managers promote trust. 7.____
B. Dropping hints or making <u>illusions</u> to things that you would like changed sometimes leads to resentment.
C. The entire unit <u>loses</u> respect for the manager and resents the reprimand.
D. Many people are <u>averse</u> to confronting problems directly; they would rather avoid them.

8. A. What does this say about the <u>effect</u> our expectations have on those we supervise? 8.____
B. In an effort to save time between 9 A.M. and 1 P.M., the staff members devised <u>their</u> own interpretation of what was to be done on these forms.
C. The task master's <u>principal</u> concern is for getting the work done; he or she is not concerned about the needs or interests of employees.
D. The advisor's main objective was increasing Angela's ability to invest her <u>capitol</u> wisely.

9. A. A typical problem is that people have to cope with the internal <u>censer</u> of their feelings. 9.____
B. Sometimes, in their attempt to sound more learned, people speak in ways that are barely <u>comprehensible</u>.
C. The <u>council</u> will meet next Friday to decide whether Abrams should continue as representative.
D. His <u>descent</u> from grace was assured by that final word.

10. A. The doctor said that John's leg had to remain <u>stationary</u> or it would not heal properly. 10.____
B. There is a city <u>ordinance</u> against parking too close to fire hydrants.
C. Meyer's problem is that he is never <u>discrete</u> when talking about office politics.
D. Mrs. Thatcher probably worked harder <u>than</u> any other British Prime Minister had ever worked.

Questions 11-20.

DIRECTIONS: For each of the following groups of sentences in Questions 11 through 20, select the sentence which is the BEST example of English usage and grammar.

11. A. She is a woman who, at age sixty, is distinctly attractive and cares about how they look. 11.____
B. It was a seemingly impossible search, and no one knew the problems better than she.
C. On the surface, they are all sweetness and light, but his morbid character is under it.
D. The minicopier, designed to appeal to those who do business on the run like architects in the field or business travelers, weigh about four pounds.

12. A. Neither the administrators nor the union representative regret the decision to settle the disagreement. 12.____
B. The plans which are made earlier this year were no longer being considered.
C. I would have rode with him if I had known he was leaving at five.
D. I don't know who she said had it.

13. A. Writing at a desk, the memo was handed to her for immediate attention. 13.____
B. Carla didn't water Carl's plants this week, which she never does.
C. Not only are they good workers, with excellent writing and speaking skills, and they get to the crux of any problem we hand them.
D. We've noticed that this enthusiasm for undertaking new projects sometimes interferes with his attention to detail.

14. A. It's obvious that Nick offends people by being unruly, inattentive, and having no patience. 14.____
B. Marcia told Genie that she would have to leave soon.
C. Here are the papers you need to complete your investigation.
D. Julio was startled by you're comment.

15. A. The new manager has done good since receiving her promotion, but her secretary has helped her a great deal. 15.____
B. One of the personnel managers approached John and tells him that the client arrived unexpectedly.
C. If somebody can supply us with the correct figures, they should do so immediately.
D. Like zealots, advocates seek power because they want to influence the policies and actions of an organization.

16. A. Between you and me, Chris probably won't finish this assignment in time. 16.____
B. Rounding the corner, the snack bar appeared before us.
C. Parker's radical reputation made to the Supreme Court his appointment impossible.
D. By the time we arrived, Marion finishes briefing James and returns to Hank's office.

17. A. As we pointed out earlier, the critical determinant of the success of middle managers is their ability to communicate well with others. 17.____
    B. The lecturer stated there wasn't no reason for bad supervision.
    C. We are well aware whose at fault in this instance.
    D. When planning important changes, it's often wise to seek the participation of others because employees often have much valuable ideas to offer.

18. A. Joan had ought to throw out those old things that were damaged when the roof leaked. 18.____
    B. I spose he'll let us know what he's decided when he finally comes to a decision.
    C. Carmen was walking to work when she suddenly realized that she had left her lunch on the table as she passed the market.
    D. Are these enough plants for your new office?

19. A. First move the lever forward, and then they should lift the ribbon casing before trying to take it out. 19.____
    B. Michael finished quickest than any other person in the office.
    C. There is a special meeting for we committee members today at 4 p.m.
    D. My husband is worried about our having to work overtime next week.

20. A. Another source of conflicts are individuals who possess very poor interpersonal skills. 20.____
    B. It is difficult for us to work with him on projects because these kinds of people are not interested in team building.
    C. Each of the departments was represented at the meeting.
    D. Poor boy, he never should of past that truck on the right.

Questions 21-28.

DIRECTIONS: In Questions 21 through 28, there may be a problem with English grammar or usage. If a problem does exist, select the letter that indicates the most effective change. If no problem exists, select choice A.

21. He rushed her to the hospital and stayed with her, even though this took quite a bit of his time, he didn't charge her anything. 21.____

    A. No changes are necessary
    B. Change <u>even though</u> to <u>although</u>
    C. Change the first comma to a period and capitalize <u>even</u>
    D. Change <u>rushed</u> to <u>had rushed</u>

22. Waiting that appears unfairly feels longer than waiting that seems justified. 22.____

    A. No changes are necessary
    B. Change <u>unfairly</u> to <u>unfair</u>
    C. Change <u>appears</u> to <u>seems</u>
    D. Change <u>longer</u> to <u>longest</u>

23. May be you and the person who argued with you will be able to reach an agreement. 23.____

    A. No changes are necessary
    B. Change will be to were
    C. Change argued with to had an argument with
    D. Change May be to Maybe

24. Any one of them could of taken the file while you were having coffee. 24.____

    A. No changes are necessary
    B. Change any one to anyone
    C. Change of to have
    D. Change were having to were out having

25. While people get jobs or move from poverty level to better paying employment, they stop receiving benefits and start paying taxes. 25.____

    A. No changes are necessary
    B. Change While to As
    C. Change stop to will stop
    D. Change get to obtain

26. Maribeth's phone rang while talking to George about the possibility of their meeting Tom at three this afternoon. 26.____

    A. No changes are necessary
    B. Change their to her
    C. Move to George so that it follows Tom
    D. Change talking to she was talking

27. According to their father, Lisa is smarter than Chris, but Emily is the smartest of the three sisters. 27.____

    A. No changes are necessary
    B. Change their to her
    C. Change is to was
    D. Make two sentences, changing the second comma to a period and omitting but

28. Yesterday, Mark and he claim that Carl took Carol's ideas and used them inappropriately. 28.____

    A. No changes are necessary
    B. Change claim to claimed
    C. Change inappropriately to inappropriate
    D. Change Carol's to Carols'

Questions 29-34.

DIRECTIONS: For each group of sentences in Questions 29 through 34, select the choice that represents the BEST editing of the problem sentence.

29. The managers expected employees to be at their desks at all times, but they would always be late or leave unannounced. 29.____

A. The managers wanted employees to always be at their desks, but they would always be late or leave unannounced.
B. Although the managers expected employees to be at their desks no matter what came up, they would always be late and leave without telling anyone.
C. Although the managers expected employees to be at their desks at all times, the managers would always be late or leave without telling anyone.
D. The managers expected the employee to never leave their desks, but they would always be late or leave without telling anyone.

30. The one who is department manager he will call you to discuss the problem tomorrow morning at 10 A.M. 30.____

A. The one who is department manager will call you tomorrow morning at ten to discuss the problem.
B. The department manager will call you to discuss the problem tomorrow at 10 A.M.
C. Tomorrow morning at 10 A.M., the department manager will call you to discuss the problem.
D. Tomorrow morning the department manager will call you to discuss the problem.

31. A conference on child care in the workplace the $200 cost of which to attend may be prohibitive to childcare workers who earn less than that weekly. 31.____

A. A conference on child care in the workplace that costs $200 may be too expensive for childcare workers who earn less than that each week.
B. A conference on child care in the workplace, the cost of which to attend is $200, may be prohibitive to childcare workers who earn less than that weekly.
C. A conference on child care in the workplace who costs $200 may be too expensive for childcare workers who earn less than that a week.
D. A conference on child care in the workplace which costs $200 may be too expensive to childcare workers who earn less than that on a weekly basis.

32. In accordance with estimates recently made, there are 40,000 to 50,000 nuclear weapons in our world today. 32.____

A. Because of estimates recently, there are 40,000 to 50,000 nuclear weapons in the world today.
B. In accordance with estimates made recently, there are 40,000 to 50,000 nuclear weapons in the world today.
C. According to estimates made recently, there are 40,000 to 50,000 weapons in the world today.
D. According to recent estimates, there are 40,000 to 50,000 nuclear weapons in the world today.

33. Motivation is important in problem solving, but they say that excessive motivation can inhibit the creative process. 33.____

A. Motivation is important in problem solving, but, as they say, too much of it can inhibit the creative process.
B. Motivation is important in problem solving and excessive motivation will inhibit the creative process.
C. Motivation is important in problem solving, but excessive motivation can inhibit the creative process.

D. Motivation is important in problem solving because excessive motivation can inhibit the creative process

34. In selecting the best option calls for consulting with all the people that are involved in it. 34.____

A. In selecting the best option consulting with all the people concerned with it.
B. Calling for the best option, we consulted all the affected people.
C. We called all the people involved to select the best option.
D. To be sure of selecting the best option, one should consult all the people involved.

35. There are a number of problems with the following letter. From the options below, select the version that is MOST in accordance with standard business style, tone, and form. 35.____

Dear Sir:

We are so sorry that we have had to backorder your order for 15,000 widgets and 2,300 whatzits for such a long time. We have been having incredibly bad luck lately. When your order first came in no one could get to it because my secretary was out with the flu and her replacement didn't know what she was doing, then there was the dock strike in Cucamonga which held things up for awhile, and then it just somehow got lost. We think it may have fallen behind the radiator.

We are happy to say that all these problems have been taken care of, we are caught up on supplies, and we should have the stuff to you soon, in the near future --about two weeks. You may not believe us after everything you've been through with us, but it's true.

We'll let you know as soon as we have a secure date for delivery. Thank you so much for continuing to do business with us after all the problems this probably has caused you.

Yours very sincerely,

Rob Barker

A. Dear Sir:

We are so sorry that we have had to backorder your order for 15,000 widgets and 2,300 whatzits. We have been having problems with staff lately and the dock strike hasn't helped anything.

We are happy to say that all these problems have been taken care of. I've told my secretary to get right on it, and we should have the stuff to you soon. Thank you so much for continuing to do business with us after all the problems this must have caused you.

We'll let you know as soon as we have a secure date for delivery.

Sincerely,

Rob Barker

B. Dear Sir:

We regret that we haven't been able to fill your order for 15,000 widgets and 2,300 whatzits in a timely fashion.

We'll let you know as soon as we have a secure date for delivery.

Sincerely,

Rob Barker

C. Dear Sir:

We are so very sorry that we haven't been able to fill your order for 15,000 widgets and 2,300 whatzits. We have been having incredibly bad luck lately, but things are much better now.

Thank you so much for bearing with us through all of this. We'll let you know as soon as we have a secure date for delivery.

Sincerely,

Rob Barker

D. Dear Sir:

We are very sorry that we haven't been able to fill your order for 15,000 widgets and 2,300 whatzits. Due to unforeseen difficulties, we have had to back-order your request. At this time, supplies have caught up to demand, and we foresee a delivery date within the next two weeks.

We'll let you know as soon as we have a secure date for delivery. Thank you for your patience.

Sincerely,

Rob Barker

KEY (CORRECT ANSWERS)

1. D
2. A
3. B
4. A
5. B

6. C
7. B
8. D
9. A
10. C

11. B
12. D
13. D
14. C
15. D

16. A
17. A
18. D
19. D
20. C

21. C
22. B
23. D
24. C
25. B

26. D
27. A
28. B
29. C
30. B

31. A
32. D
33. C
34. D
35. D

EXAMINATION SECTION

TEST 1

DIRECTIONS: Each question or incomplete statement is followed by several suggested answers or completions. Select the one that BEST answers the question or completes the statement. *PRINT THE LETTER OF THE CORRECT ANSWER IN THE SPACE AT THE RIGHT.*

Questions 1-45.

DIRECTIONS: In the passages below, at each place where there is a number below the line of text, decide what punctuation, if any, is needed there. In the questions numbered to correspond to the place in the text, locate the punctuation you consider correct for that place. (*N* means *no punctuation.*) Print the letter of the CORRECT choice in the space at the right.

An experiment in the growing of the guayule plant which may eventually prove to be a very
1 2
important source of rubber is being conducted at Salinas California.
3 4 5

1. A. N B. , C. ; 1.____
2. A. N B. , 2.____
3. A. N B. , 3.____
4. A. N B. , C. ; 4.____
5. A. N B. ,

A number of trucks will today begin moving 750 tons of equipment and office records of the
6
Employees Compensation Commission from Washington to its new headquarters in New York.
7
This agency which is the third largest government bureau to be moved out of Washington to
8 9
provide more space for essential workers in the nations capital will bring 500 employees.
10 11 12
Although the moving of the equipment is scheduled for completion this week the employees
13 14
will not begin work here until next week for it is realized that they will need some time to get
15 16
settled.

6. A. N B. n's C. ns' 6.____

7.	A. N	B. t's	C. ts'		7.____
8.	A. N	B. ,			8.____
9.	A. N	B. ,			9.____
10.	A. N	B. r's	C. rs'		10.____
11.	A. N	B. n's	C. ns'		11.____
12.	A. N	B. ,			12.____
13.	A. N	B. ,			13.____
14.	A. N	B. ,	C. ;		14.____
15.	A. N	B. ,			15.____
16.	A. N	B. ,	C. ;		16.____

Theres a short cut you can take Mrs. Adams replied if you turn off the main highway just
17 18 19 20
beyond the church but I dont think its a very good road
21 22 23 24

17.	A. N	B. “			17.____
18.	A. N	B. e's	C. es'		18.____
19.	A. ,	B. .	C. ,”	D. .”	19.____
20.	A. ,	B. .	C. ,“	D. .“	20.____
21.	A. N	B. ,			21.____
22.	A. N	B. n't	C. nt'		22.____
23.	A. N	B. t's	C. ts'		23.____
24.	A. N	B. .	C. .”		24.____

Thursday night February 16 the first total eclipse of the moon for this year will occur.
25 26
Astronomers from the Hayden Planetarium members of the Amateur Astronomers Association
27 28
and several other groups have established an observation post near Westbury.
29

25. A. N B. , 25.____

26. A. N B. , 26.____

27. A. N B. , 27.____

28. A. N B. , 28.____

29. A. N B. , 29.____

She stopped by the side of the car and turned to her companion I am afraid that I cant offer to
30 31
give you a lift Henry she said I have to stop at my mothers house and its likely that she
32 33 34 35 36
will want me to stay for a while
37

30. A. N B. , C. . D. , E. . “ 30.____

31. A. N B. n’t C. nt’ 31.____

32. A. N B. , C. . 32.____

33. A. , B. . C. ,” D. .” 33.____

34. A. , B. . C. , “ D. . “ 34.____

35. A. N B. r’s C. rs’ 35.____

36. A. N B. t’s` C. ts’ 36.____

37. A. N B. . C. .” 37.____

March is the month for deciding if one is ever to decide whether or not to have a vegetable
38 39 40
garden. Of course only the laggard waits until this season any gardener who is a real
41 42
enthusiast always starts planning his crops for next year before this years harvest is on the
43 44 45
table.

38. A. N B. , C. ; 38.____

39. A. N B. , 39.____

40. A. N B. , 40.____

41. A. N B. , C. ; 41.____

42. A. N B. , 42.____

43. A. N B. , 43.____

44. A. N B. r's C. rs' 44.____

45. A. N B. ,

Questions 46-69.

DIRECTIONS: In the passages below, study each word that has a number printed under it and decide whether the word should be capitalized. C means the word should be capitalized; S means the word should not be capitalized. Some words which should be capitalized do not have numbers under them. Do not worry about such words. You are to be concerned only with the numbered words.

Two offices in manhattan will be open all day sunday, march 15, to receive income tax
46 47 48 49
returns and payments. a full staff will be on hand at the headquarters for manhattan south of
50 51
twenty-third street, as well as at the midtown office at 110 east forty-fifth street.
52 53 54

46. A. C B. S 46.____

47. A. C B. S 47.____

48. A. C B. S 48.____

49. A. C B. S 49.____

50. A. C B. S 50.____

51. A. C B. S 51.____

52. A. C B. S 52.____

53. A. C B. S 53.____

54. A. C B. S 54.____

In the book entitled "cortez and the conquest of mexico," the story is told of how a mere
55 56 57 58
handful of spanish soldiers sailed from cuba, landed on the mexican coast, fought their way
59 60 61
to mexico city, took its ruler prisoner, and captured the city.
62 63 64

55. A. C B. S 55.____

56. A. C B. S 56.____

57. A. C B. S 57.____

58. A. C B. S 58.____

59. A. C B. S 59.____

60. A. C B. S 60.____

61. A. C B. S 61.____

62. A. C B. S 62.____

63. A. C B. S 63.____

64. A. C B. S 64.____

John walked to the door with his guest. "let me know when you are in town again, colonel
65 66
johnson," he said. "if I am not at home, my cousin will know where you can reach me."
67 68 69

65. A. C B. S 65.____

66. A. C B. S 66.____

67. A. C B. S 67.____

68. A. C B. S 68.____

69. A. C B. S 69.____

KEY (CORRECT ANSWERS)

1.	B	11.	B	21.	B	31.	B	41.	C	51.	B	61.	B
2.	A	12.	B	22.	B	32.	B	42.	A	52.	A	62.	A
3.	A	13.	A	23.	B	33.	C	43.	A	53.	A	63.	B
4.	B	14.	B	24.	C	34.	D	44.	B	54.	A	64.	B
5.	B	15.	B	25.	B	35.	B	45.	A	55.	A	65.	A
6.	A	16.	A	26.	B	36.	B	46.	A	56.	B	66.	A
7.	A	17.	B	27.	B	37.	C	47.	A	57.	A	67.	B
8.	B	18.	B	28.	B	38.	A	48.	A	58.	B	68.	A
9.	A	19.	C	29.	A	39.	B	49.	B	59.	A	69.	B
10.	A	20.	C	30.	E	40.	B	50.	A	60.	A		

TEST 2

DIRECTIONS: Read each sentence and decide whether there is an error in usage in any of the underlined parts of the sentence. If so, note the letter printed under the WRONG word or phrase and put this letter in the space at the right. If there is no usage error in the sentence, put a zero (0) in the space at the right. No sentence has more than one error, and some sentences do not have any errors. The sentences are to be judged on the basis of suitable usage for general written English.

1. Tom spent (A) that summer at the beach, where him (B) and one of his classmates were (C) employed as (D) life guards. 1.____

2. They're (A) grateful to him because (B) he gave (C) them help when they was (D) in need of it. 2.____

3. She thinks George, not you, is (A) the one who (B) sent (C) her them (D) flowers. 3.____

4. A committee of the dramatic club is (A) said to have chose (B) a very interesting play for (C) presentation in (D) May. 4.____

5. Let (A) them stay a little longer (B) if they want (C) to; let's us (D) go home. 5.____

6. Twenty years (A) ago he seen (B) the danger of (C) this course of action and warned against (D) it. 6.____

7. I was not completely (A) convinced by his (B) insisting that it was them (C) who were (D) to blame. 7.____

8. He attributes his success to (A) his custom of delegating (B) as (C) much authority as possible to people in who (D) he has confidence. 8.____

9. We stopped at the next roadside stand we came (A) to and John he (B) went (C) inside (D) to get some sandwiches. 9.____

10. He could have taken part in the final match if he hadn't of been defeated in the 10.____
A B C D
preliminary contest.

11. Something is got to be done immediately, for the situation is becoming worse, 11.____
A
and there may not be another opportunity to correct these conditions.
B C D

12. A few days before the time that us employees had chosen for our annual 12.____
A B C
picnic, a committee was appointed to make the necessary arrangements.
D

13. Mr. Green, like many others, has approached us on this question, but Alice 13.____
A B
and me really don't have anything to do with it.
C D

14. When we were about three mile from the farm, a tire blew out, and we had 14.____
A B C
to stop to put on the spare tire.
D

15. Before beginning to mix a cake, you should assemble all the ingredients 15.____
A B
that is called for in the recipe.
C D

16. The engine of the wrecked plane had tore loose from the fuselage and sunk 16.____
A B C
in twenty feet of water.
D

17. Men at all times have felt the need to fashion for theirselves some kind of 17.____
A B C D
creed to live by.

18. The Amateur Athletic Union allows the payment of the contestants' hotel 18.____
A
and traveling expenses, but doesn't permit no reimbursement for time lost
B C
from work.
D

19. They have decided to hire women for the inspection of small parts, a job at 19.____
A
which they have proved more efficient than the men who they replace.
B C D

20. My brother is two years older than I, but I never have to wear his outgrown 20.____
A B C
clothes because I am taller than him.
D

21. He asked whether the situation would of improved or seemed different if 21.____
A B
they had been better informed.
C D

22. According to the seed catalogue, this here variety of beans is very well 22.____
A B C D
suited to the small vegetable garden.

23. The pleasure he took in the work and the helpful experience were his main 23.____
A B
incentives, but of course the fifty dollars were no small prize.
C D

24. The ill-fated plane snapped off tree tops for nearly half a mile before it 24.____
A B C
bursted into flames.
D

25. If they would have known that the departure of all residents except wives and 25.____
A B
children of officers was entirely voluntary, they would have stayed.
C D

26. Most of this magazine is devoted to fiction, but there is usually two or three 26.____
A B C D
timely articles in each issue.

27. Every man, whether citizen or alien, must register their name and other 27.____
A B C
information at the local board.
D

28. It was impossible to tell whom it was that had sent the package, as there 28.____
A B C
was no return address on it.
D

29. Since the meeting began so late, there will not be time to allow each of the 29.____
A B C
members to express their own opinion.
D

30. It seems to we radio listeners that too many of the best programs are 30.____
A B
presented at the same time, and that there are many evenings when very
C
little of interest is on the air.
D

31. Barrett always use to leave his office at about six o'clock, but when I got 31.____
A B
there that day his secretary told me he had gone home a little after four.
C D

32. The amount of our liabilities has increased considerable in the last few 32.____
A B
months, according to the treasurer, and there is some question whether we
C D
can continue.

33. Perhaps the greatest merit of this novel lays in the development of the two 33.____
A
main characters and the portrayal of their effect on each other.
B C D

34. He had to postpone making the purchase on account of he didn't have 34.____
A B C
sufficient cash at the time.
D

35. At this school for mountain boys and girls, the students pay for neither 35.____
A B C
tuition or maintenance.
D

36. I remember thinking at the time that Dr. Robinson was coming to see my 36.____
A B
sister rather than me.
C D

37. Twenty years ago there was more than fifty schooners sailing out of Boston 37.____
A B C
with cargo for southern ports.
D

38. Mother had dinner waiting for my brothers and I when we got home, although 38.____
A B
it was quite late when we arrived.
C D

39. Today's announcement that mine fields have been laid around the off-shore 39.____
A B
islands was received with astonishment.
C D

40. They had drunk the last drop of water, and some who had had no sleep for 40.____
A B
thirty-six hours couldn't hardly keep their eyes open.
C D

41. In the last five years, the number of cattle owned by the Indians on this 41.____
A B C
reservation have increased from 2,000 to more than 12,000.
D

42. In this group there are many British and Norwegian refugees, which have just 42.____
A B
begun to get accustomed to their new surroundings.
C D

43. This affects you principally – at least more than it does Philip and I. 43.____
A B C D

44. You hadn't ought to believe everything you see in print, as many rumors and 44.____
A B
unconfirmed reports are being published every day.
C D

45. My father thinks that it would be best for my sister and I to stay at home this 45.____
A B C D
summer.

46. Last year, when we lived in the country, I use to take my dog for a run in the 46.____
A B C
woods every day.
D

47. The old fellow was proud of the fact that he had not run for a train or swum a 47.____
A B
river or took a hike or done a bit of work in twenty years.
C D

48. He told us that he expected to be able to report some progress in a week or 48.____
A
two, but said that we hadn't ought to be too disappointed if a longer period
B C
was required.
C

49. The supply of golf balls laid in by the various dealers for the spring and 49.____
A
winter trade are almost exhausted.
B C D

50. The manager insists that either he or one of his clerks have to be on hand 50.____
A B
throughout the day in case of an urgent order.
C D

51. We hoped to keep this matter secret while the acceptance of the new members 51.____
A B C
were being considered.
D

52. From the mountains comes news of more avalanches, which have interrupted 52.____
A B C
traffic and taken several lives.
D

53. Spring in Washington is a great time for tourists, especially school children, 53.____
A
who swarm into the all ready crowded hotels of the capital.
B C D

54. Since everyone knows that my hobby is collecting postcards, each time that 54.____
A B
any one of my friends or relatives go on a trip, I am sure to receive at least
C D
one new postcard for my collection.

55. I think that a person will probably remember a book they have read much 55.____
A B C
longer than a movie on the same subject.
D

56. The possibility of joint development of the resources of the Amazon and 56.____
A
its tributaries by the United States and Brazil was the principle topic of
B C D
discussion.

57. The organ grinder's monkey graciously excepted the coins we children 57.____
A B C
offered, and politely tipped his hat.
D

58. This writer <u>is</u> one of the few authors of fiction <u>who</u> <u>are</u> distinguished <u>for</u> artistic integrity in the short story. 58.____

(A = is, B = who, C = are, D = for)

59. Mr. Kraft, <u>whom</u> we later learned had been a farmer himself for many <u>years,</u> said that the production of truck crops in the past few months <u>has</u> been much better <u>than</u> last year. 59.____

(A = whom, B = years, C = has, D = than)

60. The experimental study and the occasional practice use of this vitamin during the past decade <u>has</u> <u>given</u> some promising results, but definite comment is withheld <u>until</u> additional data <u>are</u> available. 60.____

(A = has, B = given, C = until, D = are)

KEY (CORRECT ANSWERS)

1.	B	11.	A	21.	A	31.	A	41.	D	51.	D
2.	D	12.	B	22.	B	32.	B	42.	B	52.	0
3.	D	13.	C	23.	C	33.	A	43.	D	53.	C
4.	B	14.	B	24.	D	34.	B	44.	A	54.	C
5.	D	15.	D	25.	A	35.	D	45.	C	55.	B
6.	B	16.	A	26.	D	36.	0	46.	B	56.	D
7.	C	17.	D	27.	C	37.	C	47.	C	57.	B
8.	D	18.	C	28.	A	38.	A	48.	B	58.	0
9.	B	19.	D	29.	D	39.	0	49.	B	59.	A
10.	C	20.	D	30.	A	40.	C	50.	B	60.	A

TEST 3

DIRECTIONS: Each question or incomplete statement is followed by several suggested answers or completions. Select the one that BEST answers the question or completes the statement. *PRINT THE LETTER OF THE CORRECT ANSWER IN THE SPACE AT THE RIGHT.*

Questions 1-20.

DIRECTIONS: Different versions of each passage of prose are given in the two columns below. Choose the better version of each section and answer certain questions about the sections. First, read quickly through Column 1 of the passage to get the meaning of the whole passage. Then, compare the two different versions of each lettered section as given in Columns 1 and 2 above.

Column 1

A-1 One summer evening three men were dining together in the garden of a villa in the year 1848, in the Sabine hills, overlooking Rome.

B-1 The hidden garden in which the three men sat lay some twenty feet below the south end of the terrace, and was a steep slope planted with vineyards.

C-1 The table stood among potted orange and oleander trees, in a sanded square, shaded by spreading oaks that grew out of the rocks overhead.

D-1 Beyond the balustrade was a drop into space, and far below the landscape stretched soft and undulating; there was nothing to arrest the eye until it reached Rome itself.

Column 2

A-2 One summer evening in the year 1848, three men were dining together in the garden of a villa in the Sabine hills, overlooking Rome.

B-2 In this hidden garden sat the three men, which lay some twenty feet below the south end of the terrace, being a mere shelf of rock, overhanging a steep slope planted with vineyards.

C-2 The table standing among potted orange and oleander trees, in a sanded square, shaded by spreading oaks that grew out of the rocks overhead.

D-2 There was a drop into space beyond the balustrade, and the landscape stretched soft and undulating far below, and there was nothing to arrest the eye until it reached Rome itself.

1. Section A is better expressed in 1.____
   A. Column 1 B. Column 2

2. In the inferior version of Section A, 2.____
   A. an incomplete sentence is used
   B. the modifiers are not logically grouped
   C. there is too much repetition
   D. there is a dangling participle

3. Section B is better expressed in 3.____
   A. Column 1 B. Column 2

4. In the inferior version of Section D, 4.____
   A. the *which* clause appears to modify the wrong noun
   B. variety of structure is lacking
   C. essential words have been omitted
   D. two independent clauses are incorrectly used in a single sentence

5. Section C is better expressed in 5.____
   A. Column 1 B. Column 2

6. The inferior version of Section C is poor because 6.____
   A. there is a lack of parallel structure
   B. there is a dangling participle
   C. a part of a sentence is incorrectly used as a complete sentence
   D. the word order is confused

7. Section D is better expressed in 7.____
   A. Column 1 B. Column 2

8. The inferior version of Section D is poor because 8.____
   A. part of a sentence is punctuated as if it were a complete sentence
   B. modifiers are wrongly placed
   C. essential words have been omitted
   D. there are too many sentence elements connected by *and*

Column 1

A-1 Always in times of war or other upheaval, "Will the world ever be the same again?" is a question that is always asked.

B-1 Chateaubriand, a young French aristocrat, whose case at the time of the French Revolution may be considered.

C-1 His life was in danger; he was exiled from his native land; his friends, his brother, his King had all been beheaded; he himself was in London, starving.

D-1 He sure must have wondered if the world would ever be the same.

E-1 Moreover, he was back in France a few years later, well treated and becoming famous, his country seeming prosperous and well governed.

F-1 The world was no longer the same, that is true; but it was not worse, it was only different.

Column 2

A-2 Will the world ever be the same again? This question is always asked in times of war or other upheaval.

B-2 Consider the case of a young French aristocrat like Chateaubriand, at the time of the French Revolution.

C-2 He was exiled from his native land and his life was in danger, and they had beheaded his friends, brother, and King, and he was starving in London himself.

D-2 Well might he have asked: "Will the world ever be the same?"

E-2 A few years later, however, he was back in France, well treated and on the road to fame, and his country seemed prosperous and well governed.

F-2 Indubitably the world was no longer its previous self; but it had not actually deteriorated, it had merely altered.

9. Section A is better expressed in 9.____
   A. Column 1 B. Column 2

10. In the better version of Section A, 10.____
   A. there is more variety in the types of modifiers
   B. there is more variety of vocabulary
   C. emphasis is gained by repetition
   D. emphasis is gained by the use of two separate sentences

11. Section B is better expressed in 11.____
   A. Column 1 B. Column 2

12. In the inferior version of Section B, 12.____
   A. an incomplete sentence is used
   B. two independent clauses are incorrectly used in a single sentence
   C. modifiers are incorrectly placed
   D. the sentence structure is too monotonous

13. Section C is better expressed in 13.____
   A. Column 1 B. Column 2

14. The inferior version of Section C is poor because 14.____
   A. the word order is grammatically incorrect
   B. too many words are understood instead of expressed
   C. there are too many sentence elements joined by *and*
   D. the wording is not logical

15. Section D is better expressed in 15.____
   A. Column 1 B. Column 2

16. The inferior version of Section D is poor because 16.____
   A. inverted sentence order is used
   B. variety in sentence structure is lacking
   C. the sentence structure is confused
   D. the colloquial expression is inappropriate

17. Section E is better expressed in 17.____
   A. Column 1 B. Column 2

18. The inferior version of Section E is poor chiefly because 18.____
   A. a modifier is wrongly placed
   B. there is a dangling participle
   C. an incomplete sentence is incorrectly used
   D. the choice of connecting words is poor

19. Section F is better expressed in 19.____
   A. Column 1 B. Column 2

20. The inferior version of Section F is poor because 20.____
    A. of the use of colloquial expressions
    B. of the unnecessary avoidance of short, common words
    C. an incomplete sentence is used
    D. there is too much repetition

Questions 21-24.

DIRECTIONS: Read each of the following groups of sentences carefully; then decide which one of the four choices in each group is expressed most satisfactorily. PRINT THE LETTER OF THE CORRECT ANSWER IN THE SPACE AT THE RIGHT.

21. A. In getting the morning mail a distance of nearly half a mile must be traversed by us, this being the distance to the highway. 21.____
    B. We have to walk a distance of nearly half a mile down to the highway getting the morning mail.
    C. In order to get the morning mail we have to walk down to the highway, a distance of nearly half a mile.
    D. The highway is nearly half a mile distant and wanting to get the morning mail this distance must be walked.

22. A. From my window you can see an apple tree. It stands beyond the meadow nearly half a mile away. This apple tree is the last one of an ancient line. The line once marked the boundary between the upper and lower pastures. 22.____
    B. Beyond the meadow, nearly half a mile away, yet in sight from my window, stands an apple tree, the last of an ancient line that once marked the boundary between the upper and lower pastures.
    C. An apple tree which is the last of an ancient line of apple trees that once marked the boundary between the upper and lower pastures and which is in sight from my window, though nearly a half mile away, is beyond the meadow.
    D. An apple tree stands beyond the meadow and nearly half a mile away though in sight from my window and it is the last of an ancient line of apple trees that once marked the boundary between the upper and lower pastures.

23. A. Harry and Doris will represent our school in the debating contest, and their work as public speakers has been excellent this year. 23.____
    B. Having done excellent work as public speakers this year, our school will be represented in the debating contest by Harry and Doris.
    C. Our school will be represented in the debating contest by Harry and Doris, their work as public speakers has been excellent this year.
    D. Harry and Doris, whose work as public speakers has been excellent this year, will represent our school in the debating contest.

24. A. O. Henry's marvelous craftsmanship, which could make an expanded anecdote, ending with a sudden humorous or tragic surprise, into a perfect prose narrative, is still a model for present-day writers. 24.____
    B. O. Henry's marvelous craftsmanship, which could make an expanded anecdote, ending with a sudden humorous or tragic surprise, into a perfect prose narrative. It is still a model for present-day writers.
    C. O. Henry's marvelous craftsmanship is still a model for present-day writers, which could make an expanded anecdote, ending with a sudden humorous or tragic surprise, into a perfect prose narrative.
    D. O. Henry's marvelous craftsmanship, making an expanded anecdote, ending with a sudden humorous or tragic surprise, into a perfect prose narrative, which is still a model for present-day writers.

KEY (CORRECT ANSWERS)

1. B
2. B
3. A
4. A
5. A

6. C
7. A
8. D
9. B
10. D

11. B
12. A
13. A
14. C
15. B

16. D
17. B
18. D
19. A
20. B

21. C
22. B
23. D
24. A

WRITTEN ENGLISH EXPRESSION
EXAMINATION SECTION
TEST 1

DIRECTIONS: In each of the following groups of sentences, one of the four sentences is faulty in grammar, punctuation, or capitalization. Select the incorrect sentence in each case. *PRINT THE LETTER OF THE CORRECT ANSWER IN THE SPACE AT THE RIGHT.*

1. A. If you had stood at home and done your homework, you would not have failed in arithmetic. 1._____
   B. Her affected manner annoyed every member of the audience.
   C. How will the new law affect our income taxes?
   D. The plants were not affected by the long, cold winter, but they succumbed to the drought of summer.

2. A. He is one of the most able men who have been in the Senate. 2._____
   B. It is he who is to blame for the lamentable mistake.
   C. Haven't you a helpful suggestion to make at this time?
   D. The money was robbed from the blind man's cup.

3. A. The amount of children in this school is steadily increasing. 3._____
   B. After taking an apple from the table, she went out to play.
   C. He borrowed a dollar from me.
   D. I had hoped my brother would arrive before me.

4. A. Whom do you think I hear from every week? 4._____
   B. Who do you think is the right man for the job?
   C. Who do you think I found in the room?
   D. He is the man whom we considered a good candidate for the presidency.

5. A. Quietly the puppy laid down before the fireplace. 5._____
   B. You have made your bed; now lie in it.
   C. I was badly sunburned because I had lain too long in the sun.
   D. I laid the doll on the bed and left the room.

6. A. Sailing down the bay was a thrilling experience for me. 6._____
   B. He was not consulted about your joining the club.
   C. This story is different than the one I told you yesterday.
   D. There is no doubt about his being the best player.

7. A. He maintains there is but one road to world peace. 7._____
   B. It is common knowledge that a child sees much he is not supposed to see.
   C. Much of the bitterness might have been avoided if arbitration had been restored to earlier in the meeting.
   D. The man decided it would be advisable to marry a girl somewhat younger than him.

8. A. In this book, the incident I liked least is where the hero tries to put out the forest fire. 8.____
B. Learning a foreign language will undoubtedly give a person a better understanding of his mother tongue.
C. His actions made us wonder what he planned to do next.
D. Because of the war, we were unable to travel during the summer vacation.

9. A. The class had no sooner become interested in the lesson than the dismissal bell rang. 9.____
B. There is little agreement about the kind of world to be planned at the peace conference.
C. "Today," said the teacher, "we shall read 'The Wind in the Willows.' I am sure you'll like it."
D. The terms of the legal settlement of the family quarrel handicapped both sides for many years.

10. A. I was so surprised that I was not able to say a word. 10.____
B. She is taller than any other member of the class.
C. It would be much more preferable if you were never seen in his company.
D. We had no choice but to excuse her for being late.

KEY (CORRECT ANSWERS)

1.	A	6.	C
2.	D	7.	D
3.	A	8.	A
4.	C	9.	C
5.	A	10.	C

TEST 2

DIRECTIONS: In each of the following groups of sentences, one of the four sentences is faulty in grammar, punctuation, or capitalization. Select the incorrect sentence in each case. *PRINT THE LETTER OF THE CORRECT ANSWER IN THE SPACE AT THE RIGHT.*

1. A. Please send me these data at the earliest opportunity. 1._____
   B. The loss of their material proved to be a severe handicap.
   C. My principal objection to this plan is that it is impracticable.
   D. The doll had laid in the rain for an hour and was ruined.

2. A. The garden scissors, left out all night in the rain, were in a badly rusted condition. 2._____
   B. The girls felt bad about the misunderstanding which had arisen.
   C. Sitting near the campfire, the old man told John and I about many exciting adventures he had had.
   D. Neither of us is in a position to undertake a task of that magnitude.

3. A. The general concluded that one of the three roads would lead to the besieged city. 3._____
   B. The children didn't, as a rule, do hardly anything beyond what they were told to do.
   C. The reason the girl gave for her negligence was that she had acted on the spur of the moment.
   D. The daffodils and tulips look beautiful in that blue vase.

4. A. If I was ten years older, I should be interested in this work. 4._____
   B. Give the prize to whoever has drawn the best picture.
   C. When you have finished reading the book, take it back to the library.
   D. My drawing is as good as or better than yours.

5. A. He asked me whether the substance was animal or vegetable. 5._____
   B. An apple which is unripe should not be eaten by a child.
   C. That was an insult to me who am your friend.
   D. Some spy must of reported the matter to the enemy.

6. A. Limited time makes quoting the entire message impossible. 6._____
   B. Who did she say was going?
   C. The girls in your class have dressed more dolls this year than we.
   D. There was such a large amount of books on the floor that I couldn't find a place for my rocking chair.

7. A. What with his sleeplessness and his ill health, he was unable to assume any responsibility for the success of the meeting. 7._____
   B. If I had been born in February, I should be celebrating my birthday soon.
   C. In order to prevent breakage, she placed a sheet of paper between each of the plates when she packed them.
   D. After the spring shower, the violets smelled very sweet.

8. A. He had laid the book down very reluctantly before the end of the lesson. 8._____
   B. The dog, I am sorry to say, had lain on the bed all night.
   C. The cloth was first lain on a flat surface; then it was pressed with a hot iron.
   D. While we were in Florida, we lay in the sun until we were noticeably tanned.

9. A. If John was in New York during the recent holiday season, I have no doubt he spent most of his time with his parents. 9.____
   B. How could he enjoy the television program; the dog was barking and the baby was crying.
   C. When the problem was explained to the class, he must have been asleep.
   D. She wished that her new dress were finished so that she could go to the party.

10. A. The engine not only furnishes power but light and heat as well. 10.____
   B. You're aware that we've forgotten whose guilt was established, aren't you?
   C. Everybody knows that the woman made many sacrifices for her children.
   D. A man with his dog and gun is a familiar sight in this neighborhood.

KEY (CORRECT ANSWERS)

1.	D	6.	D
2.	C	7.	B
3.	B	8.	C
4.	A	9.	B
5.	D	10.	A

TEST 3

DIRECTIONS: Each of sentences 1 to 18 may be classified most appropriately under one of the following three categories:

A. faulty because of incorrect grammar
B. faulty because of incorrect punctuation
C. correct

Examine each sentence carefully. Then, in the space at the right, print the capital letter preceding the option which is best of the three suggested above. All incorrect sentences contain but one type of error. Consider a sentence correct if it contains none of the types of errors mentioned, even though there may be other correct ways of expressing the same thought.

1. He sent the notice to the clerk who you hired yesterday. 1.____

2. It must be admitted, however that you were not informed of this change. 2.____

3. Only the employees who have served in this grade for at least two years are eligible for promotion. 3.____

4. The work was divided equally between she and Mary. 4.____

5. He thought that you were not available at that time. 5.____

6. When the messenger returns; please give him this package. 6.____

7. The new secretary prepared, typed, addressed, and delivered, the notices. 7.____

8. Walking into the room, his desk can be seen at the rear. 8.____

9. Although John has worked here longer than she, he produces a smaller amount of work. 9.____

10. She said she could of typed this report yesterday. 10.____

11. Neither one of these procedures are adequate for the efficient performance of this task. 11.____

12. The typewriter is the tool of the typist; the cash register, the tool of the cashier. 12.____

13. "The assignment must be completed as soon as possible" said the supervisor. 13.____

14. As you know, office handbooks are issued to all new employees. 14.____

15. Writing a speech is sometimes easier than to deliver it before an audience. 15.____

16. Mr. Brown our accountant, will audit the accounts next week. 16.____

17. Give the assignment to whomever is able to do it most efficiently. 17.____

18. The supervisor expected either your or I to file these reports. 18.____

KEY (CORRECT ANSWERS)

1. A	6. B	11. A	16. B
2. B	7. B	12. C	17. A
3. C	8. A	13. B	18. A
4. A	9. C	14. C	
5. C	10. A	15. A	

TEST 4

DIRECTIONS: Each sentence may be classified most appropriately under one of the following four categories:

A. faulty because of incorrect grammar
B. faulty because of incorrect punctuation
C. faulty because of incorrect spelling
D. correct

Examine each sentence carefully. Then, in the space at the right, write the capital letter preceding the best of the four alternatives suggested above. All incorrect sentences contain but one type of error. Consider a sentence correct if it contains none of the types of errors mentioned, even though there may be other correct ways of expressing the same thought.

1. The fire apparently started in the storeroom, which is usually locked. 1.____

2. On approaching the victim two bruises were noticed by this officer. 2.____

3. The officer, who was there examined the report with great care. 3.____

4. Each employee in the office had a seperate desk. 4.____

5. All employees including members of the clerical staff, were invited to the lecture. 5.____

6. The suggested procedure is similar to the one now in use. 6.____

7. No one was more pleased with the new procedure than the chauffeur. 7.____

8. He tried to pursuade her to change the procedure. 8.____

9. The total of the expenses charged to petty cash were high. 9.____

10. An understanding between him and I was finally reached. 10.____

KEY (CORRECT ANSWERS)

1. D
2. A
3. B
4. C
5. B
6. D
7. D
8. C
9. A
10. A

TEST 5

Questions 1-5.

DIRECTIONS: Each of sentences 1 to 5 may be classified under one of the following four categories:

A. faulty because of incorrect grammar
B. faulty because of incorrect punctuation
C. faulty because of incorrect capitalization or incorrect spelling
D. correct

Examine each sentence carefully to determined under which of the above four options it is best classified. Then, in the space at the right, print the capital letter preceding the option which is the best of the four suggested above. Each faulty sentence contains but one type of error. Consider a sentence to be correct if it contains none of the types of errors mentioned, even though there may be other correct ways of expressing the same thought.

1. They told both he and I that the prisoner had escaped. 1.____

2. Any superior officer, who, disregards the just complaints of his subordinates, is remiss in the performance of his duty. 2.____

3. Only those members of the national organization who resided in the Middle West attended the conference in Chicago. 3.____

4. We told him to give the investigation assignment to whoever was available. 4.____

5. Please do not disappoint and embarass us by not appearing in court. 5.____

Questions 6-10.

DIRECTIONS: Each of questions 6 to 10 consists of a sentence. Read each sentence carefully and then write your answer to each question according to the following scheme:

A. sentence contains an error in spelling only
B. sentence contains an error in grammar or word usage only
C. sentence contains one error in spelling and one error in grammar or word usage
D. sentence is correct; contains no errors

6. Although the officer's speech proved to be entertaining, the topic was not relevant to the main theme of the conference. 6.____

7. In Febuary all new officers attended a training course in which they were learned their principal duties and the fundamental operating procedures of the department. 7.____

8. I personally seen inmate Jones threaten inmates Smith and Green with bodily harm if they refused to participate in the plot. 8.____

9. To the layman, who on a chance visit to the prison observes everything functioning smoothly, the maintenance of prison discipline may seem to be a relatively easily realizable objective. 9.____

10. The prisoners in cell block fourty were forbidden to lay on the cell cots during the recreation hour. 10.____

KEY (CORRECT ANSWERS)

1.	A	6.	D
2.	B	7.	C
3.	C	8.	B
4.	D	9.	D
5.	C	10.	C

TEST 6

DIRECTIONS: Each of the following sentences may be classified under one of the following four categories:

A. faulty because of incorrect grammar
B. faulty because of incorrect punctuation
C. faulty because of incorrect capitalization or incorrect spelling
D. correct

Examine each sentence carefully to determine under which of the above four options it is best classified. Then, in the space at the right, print the capital letter preceding the option which is the best of the four suggested above. Each faulty sentence contains but one type of error. Consider a sentence to be correct if it contains none of the types of errors mentioned, even though there may be other correct ways of expressing the same thought.

1. I cannot encourage you any. 1._____
2. You always look well in those sort of clothes. 2._____
3. Shall we go to the park? 3._____
4. The man whome he introduced was Mr. Carey. 4._____
5. She saw the letter laying here this morning. 5._____
6. It should rain before the Afternoon is over. 6._____
7. They have already went home. 7._____
8. That Jackson will be elected is evident. 8._____
9. He does not hardly approve of us. 9._____
10. It was he, who won the prize. 10._____

KEY (CORRECT ANSWERS)

1.	A	6.	C
2.	A	7.	A
3.	D	8.	D
4.	C	9.	A
5.	A	10.	B

TEST 7

DIRECTIONS: Each of the following sentences may be classified under one of the following four categories:

A. faulty because of incorrect grammar
B. faulty because of incorrect punctuation
C. faulty because of incorrect capitalization or incorrect spelling
D. correct

Examine each sentence carefully to determine under which of the above four options is best classified. Then, in the space at the right, print the capital letter preceding the option which is the best of the four suggested above. Each faulty sentence contains but one type of error. Consider a sentence to be correct if it contains none of the types of errors mentioned, even though there may be other correct ways of expressing the same thought.

1. Shall we go to the park. 1._____

2. They are, alike, in this particular. 2._____

3. They gave the poor man sume food when he knocked on the door. 3._____

4. I regret the loss caused by the error. 4._____

5. The students' will have a new teacher. 5._____

6. They sweared to bring out all the facts. 6._____

7. He decided to open a branch store on 33rd street. 7._____

8. His speed is equal and more than that of a racehorse. 8._____

9. He felt very warm on that Summer day. 9._____

10. He was assisted by his friend, who lives in the next house. 10._____

KEY (CORRECT ANSWERS)

1.	B	6.	A
2.	B	7.	C
3.	C	8.	A
4.	D	9.	C
5.	B	10.	D

TEST 8

DIRECTIONS: Each of the following sentences may be classified under one of the following four categories:

A. faulty because of incorrect grammar
B. faulty because of incorrect punctuation
C. faulty because of incorrect capitalization or incorrect spelling
D. correct

Examine each sentence carefully to determine under which of the above four options it is best classified. Then, in the space at the right, print the capital letter preceding the option which is the best of the four suggested above. Each faulty sentence contains but one type of error. Consider a sentence to be correct if it contains none of the types of errors mentioned, even though there may be other correct ways of expressing the same thought.

1. The climate of New York is colder than California. 1.____

2. I shall wait for you on the corner. 2.____

3. Did we see the boy who, we think, is the leader. 3.____

4. Being a modest person, John seldom talks about his invention. 4.____

5. The gang is called the smith street boys. 5.____

6. He seen the man break into the store. 6.____

7. We expected to lay still there for quite a while. 7.____

8. He is considered to be the Leader of his organization. 8.____

9. Although I recieved an invitation, I won't go. 9.____

10. The letter must be here some place. 10.____

KEY (CORRECT ANSWERS)

1. A	6. A
2. D	7. A
3. B	8. C
4. D	9. C
5. C	10. A

TEST 9

DIRECTIONS: Each of the following sentences may be classified under one of the following four categories:

A. faulty because of incorrect grammar
B. faulty because of incorrect punctuation
C. faulty because of incorrect capitalization or incorrect spelling
D. correct

Examine each sentence carefully to determine under which of the above four options it is best classified. Then, in the space at the right, print the capital letter preceding the option which is the best of the four suggested above. Each faulty sentence contains but one type of error. Consider a sentence to be correct if it contains none of the types of errors mentioned, even though there may be other correct ways of expressing the same thought.

1. I thought it to be he. 1.____

2. We expect to remain here for a long time. 2.____

3. The committee was agreed. 3.____

4. Two-thirds of the building are finished. 4.____

5. The water was froze. 5.____

6. Everyone of the salesmen must supply their own car. 6.____

7. Who is the author of Gone With The Wind? 7.____

8. He marched on and declaring that he would never surrender. 8.____

9. Who shall I say called? 9.____

10. Everyone has left but they. 10.____

KEY (CORRECT ANSWERS)

1.	A	6.	A
2.	D	7.	B
3.	A	8.	A
4.	A	9.	D
5.	A	10.	D

TEST 10

DIRECTIONS: Each of the following sentences may be classified under one of the following four categories:

A. faulty because of incorrect grammar
B. faulty because of incorrect punctuation
C. faulty because of incorrect capitalization or incorrect spelling
D. correct

Examine each sentence carefully to determine under which of the above four options it is best classified. Then, in the space at the right, print the capital letter preceding the option which is the best of the four suggested above. Each faulty sentence contains but one type of error. Consider a sentence to be correct if it contains none of the types of errors mentioned, even though there may be other correct ways of expressing the same thought.

1. Who did we give the order to? 1.____

2. Send your order in immediately. 2.____

3. I believe I paid the Bill. 3.____

4. I have not met but one person. 4.____

5. Why aren't Tom, and Fred, going to the dance? 5.____

6. What reason is there for him not going? 6.____

7. The seige of Malta was a tremendous event. 7.____

8. I was there yesterday I assure you. 8.____

9. Your ukelele is better than mine. 9.____

10. No one was there only Mary. 10.____

KEY (CORRECT ANSWERS)

1.	A	6.	A
2.	D	7.	C
3.	C	8.	B
4.	A	9.	C
5.	B	10.	A

WRITTEN ENGLISH EXPRESSION

EXAMINATION SECTION
TEST 1

DIRECTIONS: In each of the sentences below, four portions are underlined and lettered. Read each sentence and decide whether any of the underlined parts contains an error in spelling, punctuation, or capitalization, or employs grammatical usage which would be inappropriate for carefully written English. If so, note the letter printed under the unacceptable form and print it in the space at the right. If all four of the underlined portions are acceptable as they stand, print the letter E. No sentence contains more than one unacceptable form.

1. A low ceiling is when the atmospheric conditions make flying inadvisable. 1.____
A B C D

2. They couldn't tell who the card was from. 2.____
A B C D

3. No one but you and I are to help him. 3.____
A B C D

4. To him fall the duties of foster parent. 4.____
A B C D

5. If the world should somehow find peace within itself, so that all her people would stop fighting everlastingly...that would be the day! 5.____
A B C D

6. Every one of the teachers prepared his lessons in a consumate manner. 6.____
A B C D

7. Didn't they used to pay promptly? 7.____
A B C D

8. The services rendered by these people and their share in making the work a success is to be commended. 8.____
A B C D

9. They (A) couldn't (B) tell whom (C) the cable was recieved (D) from. 9.____

10. We like these (A) better (B) than those (C) kind. (D) 10.____

11. It (A) is a test (B) of you more (C) than I. (D) 11.____

12. The person (A) in charge being (B) him (C) there can be no change in (D) policy. 12.____

13. A large (A) amount (B) of information and news are (C) to be found there. (D) 13.____

14. I should have liked (A) to have seen (B) it (C) again. (D) 14.____

15. The desire to travel (A) made (B) him (C) restless (D) 15.____

16. Should (A) that effect (B) their (C) decision? (D) 16.____

17. Do (A) as (B) we do (C) for the celebration of the childrens' (D) event. 17.____

18. Do (A) either (B) of you (C) care (D) to join us? 18.____

19. A child's (A) food requirements (B) differ (C) from the adult (D) 19.____

20. A large family, (A) including (B) two uncles and four grandparents, live (C) at (D) the hotel. 20.____

21. If they would have done (A) that, (B) they (C) might have (D) succeeded. 21.____

22. Neither (A) the hot days or (B) the humid nights annoy (C) our (D) Southern visitor. 22.____

23. Some (A) people do not gain favor (B) because (C) they are kind of (D) tactless. 23.____

24. No sooner (A) had the turning point come (B) than (C) a new embarassing (D) issue arose. 24.____

25. An usher seldom (A) rises (B) above (C) a theatre manager (D). 25.____

KEY (CORRECT ANSWERS)

1. B
2. C
3. B
4. E
5. C

6. D
7. C
8. D
9. D
10. C

11. D
12. C
13. C
14. B
15. E

16. B
17. D
18. A
19. D
20. C

21. A
22. B
23. D
24. D
25. C

TEST 2

DIRECTIONS: In each of the sentences below, four portions are underlined and lettered. Read each sentence and decide whether any of the underlined parts contains an error in spelling, punctuation, or capitalization, or employs grammatical usage which would be inappropriate for carefully written English. If so, note the letter printed under the unacceptable form and print it in the space at the right. If all four of the underlined portions are acceptable as they stand, print the letter E. No sentence contains more than one unacceptable form.

1. The epic, "Gone With the Wind," deals with events that ocurred during the Civil War era. 1.____

A: epic, — B: , — C: ocurred — D: era.

2. Shall you be at home, let us say, on Sunday at two o'clock? 2.____

A: Shall — B: be — C: at home, — D: let us say

3. We see Mr. Lewis' take his car out of the garage daily. 3.____

A: see — B: Lewis' — C: take — D: out of the garage

4. We have no place to keep our rubbers, only in the hall closet. 4.____

A: have — B: no — C: to keep — D: only

5. Isn't it true what you told me about the best way to prepare for an examination? 5.____

A: Isn't it — B: what — C: you — D: told

6. "Who shall I say called," the butler asked ? 6.____

A: "Who — B: shall — C: asked — D: ?

7. The museum is often visited by students who are fond of Primitive paintings, and by patent attorneys. 7.____

A: is — B: are — C: Primitive — D: patent

8. I rose to nominate the superintendant, the man who most of us felt was the best. 8.____

A: rose — B: to nominate — C: superintendant, — D: who

9. The child was (A) sent to the store to purchase (B) a bottle of milk and brought (C) home fresh rolls, too. (D) 9.____

10. The garden tool was sent (A) to be sharpened (B) and a new handle to be (C) put on. (D) 10.____

11. At the end of her vacation, Joan came home with little money , (A) nevertheless (B) , (C) it was a joyous occasion. (D) 11.____

12. We people (A) have opportunities (B) to show the rest of the world how real democracy functions and leads (C) to the perfectability (D) of man. 12.____

13. The guide paddled along and then fell into (A) a reverie (B) where (C) he related (D) the history of the region. 13.____

14. We should have (A) investigated the cause of (B) the noise in the Hotel (C) by bringing (D) the car to a halt. 14.____

15. The first few strokes of the brush were (A) enough to convince (B) me that Tom could paint much better (C) than me. (D) 15.____

16. We inquired whether (A) we could see (B) the owner of the store, after we waited (C) for one hour. (D) 16.____

17. The irratation of the high-strung parent was aggravated by the slightest noise that 17.____
A B C
the baby made.
D

18. There is a large demand for men interested in the field of 18.____
A B C
Information Retrieval.
D

19. Snow after the rains delay the coming crops. 19.____
A B C D

20. They intend to partially do away with ceremonies. 20.____
A B C D

21. If that be done and turns out badly we shall see horror. 21.____
A B C D

22. The new plant is to be electrically lighted; increasing brightness by 50%. 22.____
A B C D

23. The reason the speaker was offended was that the audience was inattentive. 23.____
A B C D

24. There appear to be conditions that govern the behavioral Sciences. 24.____
A B C D

25. Either of the men are influential enough to control the situation. 25.____
A B C D

KEY (CORRECT ANSWERS)

1. C
2. E
3. B
4. D
5. B

6. D
7. C
8. C
9. C
10. C

11. A
12. D
13. C
14. C
15. D

16. C
17. A
18. D
19. C
20. E

21. C
22. C
23. E
24. D
25. B

TEST 3

DIRECTIONS: In each of the sentences below, four portions are underlined and lettered. Read each sentence and decide whether any of the underlined parts contains an error in spelling, puncutation, or capitalization, or employs grammatical usage which would be inappropriate for carefully written English. If so, note the letter printed under the unacceptable form and print it in the space at the right. If all four of the underlined portions are acceptable as they stand, print the letter E. No sentence contains more than one unacceptable form.

1. Who (A) did (B) you predict would win (C) the election this (D) year? 1.____

2. It (A) takes a lot (B) more (C) effort to sell (D) houses this year than last year. 2.____

3. Having pranced (A) into the arena with little grace and unsteady hoof (B) for the jumps ahead, (C) the driver reined his horse. (D) 3.____

4. Once the dog wagged it's (A) tail, you (B) knew it (C) was (D) a friendly animal. 4.____

5. The record of the winning team was among (A) the most (B) noteworthy (C) of the season. (D) 5.____

6. When (A) asked (B) to choose corn, cabbage, or (C) potatoes, the diner selected the latter. (D) 6.____

7. The maid wasn't (A) so (B) small that (C) she couldn't (D) reach the top window for cleaning. 7.____

8. Many people feel that powdered coffee produces a really abhorent flavor. 8.____
A B C D

9. Would you mind me trying that coat on for size? 9.____
A B C D

10. This chair looks much different than the chair we selected in the store. 10.____
A B C D

11. After trying unsuccessfully to land a job in the city, Will settled in the coun- 11.____
A B C D
try on a farm.

12. On the last attempt, the pole-vaulter came nearly to getting hurt. 12.____
A B C D

13. The observance of armistice day throughout the world offers an opportunity 13.____
A B C
to reflect on the horrors of war.
D

14. Outside of the mistakes in spelling, the child's letter was a very good one. 14.____
A B C D

15. Scisors are always dangerous for a child to handle. 15.____
A B C D

16. I assure you that I will not yield to pressure to sell my interest. 16.____
A B C D

17. Ask him if he recalls the incident which tookplace at our first meeting. 17.____
A B C D

18. The manager felt like as not to order his usher - captain to surrender his uniform. 18.____
A B C D

19. The mother of the bride climaxed (A) the occasion (B) by exlaiming, (C) "I want my children should (D) be happy forever." 19.____

20. We read (A) in the papers (B) where (C) the prospects for peace are (D) improving. 20.____

21. "Can (A) I share (B) the cab (C) with you?" was (D) frequently heard during the period of gas rationing. 21.____

22. Had (A) the police suspected (B) the ruse, they would have taken (C) relevent (D) precautions. 22.____

23. The teacher admonished the other (A) students neither (B) to speak to John, nor (C) should they (D) annoy him. 23.____

24. Fortunately, we had been told (A) that (B) there was but (C) one availible (D) service station in that area. 24.____

25. We haven't (A) hardly (B) enough (C) time to make (D) it. 25.____

KEY (CORRECT ANSWERS)

1.	E	11.	B
2.	B	12.	B
3.	D	13.	B
4.	A	14.	A
5.	E	15.	A
6.	D	16.	E
7.	B	17.	B
8.	D	18.	B
9.	B	19.	D
10.	A	20.	C

21.	A
22.	D
23.	D
24.	D
25.	A

TEST 4

DIRECTIONS: In each of the sentences below, four portions are underlined and lettered. Read each sentence and decide whether any of the underlined parts contains an error in spelling, punctuation, or capitalization, or employs grammatical usage which would be inappropriate for carefully written English. If so, note the letter printed under the unacceptable form and print it in the space at the right. If all four of the underlined portions are acceptable as they stand, print the letter E. No sentence contains more than one unacceptable form.

1. He either will fail in his attempt or will seek other Government employment. 1.____

1. He	either	will fail	in his attempt	or	will seek other	Government	employment.
	A	B		C		D	

2. After each side gave their version, the case was closed. 2.____

2.	After	each side	gave	their	version, the case	was	closed.
	A		B	C		D	

3. Every one of the cars were tagged by the police. 3.____

3.	Every	one	of the cars	were	tagged	by the police.
	A	B		C	D	

4. They can't seem to see it when I explain the theory. 4.____

4. They	can't	seem	to see	it	when I explain the theory.
	A	B	C	D	

5. It is difficult to find the genuine signature between all those submitted. 5.____

5.	It	is difficult	to find	the genuine signature	between	all	those	submitted.
	A		B		C		D	

6. She can't understand why they don't remember who to give the letter to . 6.____

6. She can't understand why	they	don't remember	who	to give the letter	to	.
	A	B	C		D	

7. Every man and woman in America is interested in his tax bill. 7.____

7.	Every	man and woman	in America	is	interested in	his	tax bill.
	A	B		C		D	

8. A guard was called to prevent them carrying away souvenirs. 8.____

8. A guard	was called	to prevent	them	carrying away	souvenirs.
	A	B	C	D	

9. Neither you nor I am to blame for the sudden slump in business. 9.____

9.	Neither	you	nor	I	am	to blame for the sudden slump in business.
	A		B	C	D	

2 (#4)

10. To you and him belong the credit. 10.____
A B C D

11. The auctioneer had less items to sell this year than last year. 11.____
A B C D

12. Theirs instead of his instructions will be followed. 12.____
A B C D

13. It is the same at his local broker's Frank Smith. 13.____
A B C D

14. The teacher politely requested each pupil to step in the room. 14.____
A B C D

15. Too many parents leave their children do as they please. 15.____
A B C D

16. He arrived safe, his papers untouched, his composure unrufled. 16.____
A B C D

17. I do not have any faith in John running for office. 17.____
A B C D

18. The musicians began to play tunefully ; keeping the proper tempo indicated for the selection. 18.____
A B C D

19. Mary' s maid of honor bought the kind of an outfit suitable for an afternoon wedding. 19.____
A B C D

20. After the debate, every one of the Speakers realized that, given another chance, he could have done better. 20.____
A B C D

21. The reason given (A) by the physician for the patient's trouble was (B) because (C) of his poor eating habits. (D) 21.____

22. The fog was so thick (A) that the driver couldn't (B) hardly (C) see more than ten feet ahead. (D) 22.____

23. I suggest that you present (A) the medal to who (B) you deem (C) best. (D) 23.____

24. A decision made by a man without much deliberation (A) is sometimes no (B) different than (C) a slow one. (D) 24.____

25. By the time (A) Jones graduates from (B) Dental School, (C) he will be (D) twenty-six years of age. 25.____

KEY (CORRECT ANSWERS)

1. D	11. A
2. C	12. A
3. C	13. D
4. C	14. D
5. C	15. B
6. C	16. D
7. E	17. C
8. C	18. B
9. E	19. C
10. C	20. B

21. C
22. B
23. B
24. D
25. C

TEST 5

Questions 1-18.

DIRECTIONS: Each of the sentences numbered 1 to 18 may be classified most appropriately under one of the following three categories:

A. faulty because of incorrect grammar
B. faulty because of incorrect punctuation
C. correct

Examine each sentence carefully. Then, in the space at the right, print the letter preceding the option which is best of those suggested above. All incorrect sentences contain but one type of error. Consider a sentence correct if it contains none of the types of errors mentioned, even though there may be other correct ways of expressing the same thought.

1. He sent the notice to the clerk who you hired yesterday. 1.____
2. It must be admitted, however that you were not informed of this change. 2.____
3. Only the employees who have served in this grade for at least two years are eligible for promotion. 3.____
4. The work was divided equally between she and Mary. 4.____
5. He thought that you were not available at that time. 5.____
6. When the messenger returns; please give him this package. 6.____
7. The new secretary prepared, typed, addressed, and delivered, the notices. 7.____
8. Walking into the room, his desk can be seen at the rear. 8.____
9. Although John has worked here longer than she, he produces a smaller amount of work. 9.____
10. She said she could of typed this report yesterday. 10.____
11. Neither one of these procedures are adequate for the efficient performance of this task. 11.____
12. The typewriter is the tool of the typist; the cash register, the tool of the cashier. 12.____
13. "The assignment must be completed as soon as possible" said the supervisor. 13.____
14. As you know, office handbooks are issued to all new employees. 14.____
15. Writing a speech is sometimes easier than to deliver it before an audience. 15.____
16. Mr. Brown our accountant, will audit the accounts next week. 16.____
17. Give the assignment to whomever is able to do it most efficiently. 17.____
18. The supervisor expected either your or I to file these reports. 18.____

Questions 19-28.

DIRECTIONS: Each of the following sentences may be classified most appropriately under one of the following four categories:

A. faulty because of incorrect grammar
B. faulty because of incorrect punctuation
C. faulty because of incorrect spelling
D. correct

Examine each sentence carefully. Then, in the space at the right, print the letter preceding the option which is best of those suggested above. All incorrect sentences contain but one type of error. Consider a sentence correct if it contains none of the types of errors mentioned, even though there may be other correct ways of expressing the same thought.

19. The fire apparently started in the storeroom, which is usually locked. 19.____

20. On approaching the victim two bruises were noticed by this officer. 20.____

21. The officer, who was there examined the report with great care. 21.____

22. Each employee in the office had a separate desk. 22.____

23. All employees including members of the clerical staff, were invited to the lecture. 23.____

24. The suggested procedure is similar to the one now in use. 24.____

25. No one was more pleased with the new procedure than the chauffeur. 25.____

26. He tried to pursuade her to change the procedure. 26.____

27. The total of the expenses charged to petty cash were high. 27.____

28. An understanding between him and I was finally reached. 28.____

KEY (CORRECT ANSWERS)

1. A
2. B
3. C
4. A
5. C
6. B
7. B
8. A
9. C
10. A
11. A
12. C
13. B
14. C
15. A
16. B
17. A
18. A
19. D
20. A
21. B
22. C
23. B
24. D
25. D
26. C
27. A
28. A

TESTS IN SPELLING

EXAMINATION SECTION
TEST 1

DIRECTIONS: In each question of the following tests, select the letter of the one MISSPELLED word in each of the listed groups of five (5) words. *PRINT THE LETTER OF THE CORRECT ANSWER IN THE SPACE AT THE RIGHT.*

1.	A. break	B. scenary	C. business	D. arouse	E. religious	1.____
2.	A. rinsed	B. height	C. jewel	D. furtile	E. doesn't	2.____
3.	A. perform	B. divide	C. apologize	D. occasion	E. acheive	3.____
4.	A. asending	B. benefit	C. disappear	D. operate	E. grammar	4.____
5.	A. forty	B. precede	C. annuel	D. parable	E. curiosity	5.____
6.	A. irritable	B. stupefy	C. gaseous	D. millionair	E. luscious	6.____
7.	A. invincible	B. Slav	C. supersede	D. haddock	E. fatigueing	7.____
8.	A. scissors	B. explanatory	C. bituminus	D. heifer	E. cessation	8.____
9.	A. caramel	B. Wisconsin	C. acquarium	D. sterilize	E. pseudonym	9.____
10.	A. precipise	B. knapsack	C. brilliance	D. challenge	E. decrepit	10.____
11.	A. certificate	B. ajourn	C. apparel	D. aggression	E. symphony	11.____
12.	A. Norwegian	B. constent	C. interruption	D. wouldn't	E. article	12.____
13.	A. heros	B. logical	C. guarantee	D. imprison	E. legitimate	13.____
14.	A. happiness	B. weird	C. miscella-neous	D. village	E. arguement	14.____
15.	A. wretched	B. tendency	C. controver-siel	D. arbitrary	E. denial	15.____
16.	A. lonliness	B. safeguard	C. pilot	D. chiefs	E. obstacle	16.____
17.	A. shining	B. profes-sional	C. scheme	D. excitment	E. expectancy	17.____
18.	A. negative	B. editorial	C. clothe	D. economize	E. suprising	18.____
19.	A. illegal	B. opinion	C. discription	D. rationalize	E. picnicking	19.____
20.	A. circuit	B. sponser	C. exasperate	D. volume	E. valuable	20.____

KEY (CORRECT ANSWERS)

1.	B.	scenery
2.	D.	fertile
3.	E.	achieve
4.	A.	ascending
5.	C.	annual
6.	D.	millionaire
7.	E.	fatiguing
8.	C.	bituminous
9.	C.	aquarium
10.	A.	precipice
11.	B.	adjourn
12.	B.	constant
13.	A.	heroes
14.	E.	argument
15.	C.	controversial
16.	A.	loneliness
17.	D.	excitement
18.	E.	surprising
19.	C.	description
20.	B.	sponsor

TEST 2

DIRECTIONS: In each question of the following tests, select the letter of the one MISSPELLED word in each of the listed groups of five (5) words. *PRINT THE LETTER OF THE CORRECT ANSWER IN THE SPACE AT THE RIGHT.*

1.	A. procession	B. perfor-mance	C. poize	D. allied	E. discipline	1.____
2.	A. advocate	B. saleries	C. commercial	D. expense	E. forcibly	2.____
3.	A. enormous	B. enterprise	C. florist	D. humilliate	E. careful	3.____
4.	A. treachery	B. bolstor	C. simplify	D. revelation	E. reciprocal	4.____
5.	A. witness	B. derisive	C. typewriter	D. relative	E. medecine	5.____
6.	A. betrayel	B. forsaken	C. impetuous	D. finesse	E. recognize	6.____
7.	A. forcast	B. pastime	C. several	D. ridiculous	E. cleanliness	7.____
8.	A. correspond	B. conceited	C. implies	D. receptacle	E. amatuer	8.____
9.	A. captain	B. definitely	C. credited	D. cordially	E. couragous	9.____
10.	A. parallel	B. various	C. obnoxious	D. assurence	E. grateful	10.____
11.	A. feirce	B. ascent	C. allies	D. doctor	E. coming	11.____
12.	A. hopeless	B. absense	C. foretell	D. certain	E. similar	12.____
13.	A. advise	B. muscle	C. manual	D. provocation	E. copywright	13.____
14.	A. behooves	B. reservoir	C. frostbiten	D. squalor	E. ambuscade	14.____
15.	A. systematic	B. precious	C. tremen-duous	D. insulation	E. brilliant	15.____
16.	A. significant	B. jurisdiction	C. libel	D. monkies	E. legacy	16.____
17.	A. delicates-sen	B. occupansy	C. gorgeous	D. consolation	E. anxiety	17.____
18.	A. tyranny	B. perennial	C. catagory	D. inspector	E. confidential	18.____
19.	A. symbol	B. formerly	C. warring	D. caution	E. bankrupcy	19.____
20.	A. aperture	B. cellaphane	C. diagnosis	D. intestinal	E. mahogany	20.____

KEY (CORRECT ANSWERS)

1. C. poise
2. B. salaries
3. D. humiliate
4. B. bolster
5. E. medicine
6. A. betrayal
7. A. forecast
8. E. amateur
9. E. courageous
10. D. assurance
11. A. fierce
12. B. abscence
13. E. copyright
14. C. frostbitten
15. C. tremendous
16. D. monkeys
17. B. occupancy
18. C. category
19. E. bankruptcy
20. B. cellophane

TEST 3

DIRECTIONS: In each question of the following tests, select the letter of the one MISSPELLED word in each of the listed groups of five (5) words. *PRINT THE LETTER OF THE CORRECT ANSWER IN THE SPACE AT THE RIGHT.*

1.	A. pitiful	B. latter	C. ommitted	D. agreement	E. reconcile	1.____
2.	A. banaana	B. routine	C. likewise	D. indecent	E. habitually	2.____
3.	A. relieve	B. copys	C. ninety	D. crowded	E. electoral	3.____
4.	A. adviseable	B. illustrative	C. financial	D. neverthe-less	E. chimneys	4.____
5.	A. prisioner	B. immediate	C. statistics	D. surgeon	E. treachery	5.____
6.	A. option	B. extradite	C. comparitive	D. jealousy	E. illusion	6.____
7.	A. handicaped	B. assurance	C. sympathy	D. speech	E. dining	7.____
8.	A. recom-mend	B. carraige	C. disapprove	D. indepen-dent	E. mortgage	8.____
9.	A. systematic	B. ingenuity	C. tenet	D. uncanny	E. intrigueing	9.____
10.	A. arduous	B. hideous	C. fervant	D. companies	E. breach	10.____
11.	A. together	B. attempt	C. loyality	D. innocent	E. rinse	11.____
12.	A. argueing	B. emergency	C. kindergar-ten	D. religious	E. schedule	12.____
13.	A. society	B. anticipate	C. dissatisfy	D. respons-able	E. temporary	13.____
14.	A. chaufeur	B. grammar	C. planned	D. dining room	E. accurate	14.____
15.	A. confidence	B. maturity	C. aspiration	D. evasion	E. insurence	15.____
16.	A. unneces-sary	B. dirigible	C. transparant	D. similar	E. appetite	16.____
17.	A. regional	B. slimy	C. tumbler	D. educator	E. femenine	17.____
18.	A. orchestra-tion	B. proclama-tion	C. pretext	D. rearme-ment	E. invoice	18.____
19.	A. fragrant	B. indepen-dent	C. halves	D. parallel	E. advanta-gous	19.____
20.	A. champion-ing	B. conversion	C. predomi-nent	D. puppet	E. anarchist	20.____

KEY (CORRECT ANSWERS)

1. C. omitted
2. A. banana
3. B. copies
4. A. advisable
5. A. prisoner
6. C. comparative
7. A. handicapped
8. B. carriage
9. E. intriguing
10. C. fervent
11. C. loyalty
12. A. arguing
13. D. responsible
14. A. chauffeur
15. E. insurance
16. C. transparent
17. E. feminine
18. D. rearmament
19. E. advantageous
20. C. predominant

TEST 4

DIRECTIONS: In each question of the following tests, select the letter of the one MISSPELLED word in each of the listed groups of five (5) words. *PRINT THE LETTER OF THE CORRECT ANSWER IN THE SPACE AT THE RIGHT.*

1.	A. wrist	B. welfare	C. necessity	D. scenery	E. tendancy	1.____
2.	A. commiting	B. accusation	C. endurance	D. agreeable	E. excitable	2.____
3.	A. despair	B. surgury	C. privilege	D. apprecia-tion	E. journeying	3.____
4.	A. cameos	B. propa-ganda	C. delicious	D. heathen	E. interupt	4.____
5.	A. relieve	B. disappear	C. develop-ment	D. matress	E. ninety-nine	5.____
6.	A. finally	B. bulitin	C. doctor	D. desirable	E. sincerely	6.____
7.	A. wrest	B. array	C. auspices	D. sacrafice	E. genera-tions	7.____
8.	A. liquid	B. vegetable	C. silence	D. familiar	E. fasinate	8.____
9.	A. tomato	B. suspence	C. leisure	D. license	E. permanent	9.____
10.	A. characteris-tic	B. soliciting	C. repititious	D. immedi-ately	E. extravagant	10.____
11.	A. travel	B. conductor	C. equiping	D. proposal	E. twofold	11.____
12.	A. philosopher	B. minority	C. manag-ment	D. emergency	E. bibliogra-phy	12.____
13.	A. construc-tive	B. employee	C. stalwart	D. masterpe-ice	E. theoretical	13.____
14.	A. dissappoint	B. volcanic	C. illiterate	D. myth	E. superficial	14.____
15.	A. totally	B. penninsula	C. sandwich	D. ripening	E. salvation	15.____
16.	A. pastel	B. aisle	C. primarly	D. journalistic	E. diminished	16.____
17.	A. warrier	B. unification	C. enamel	D. defendant	E. sustained	17.____
18.	A. incidental	B. lubricent	C. conversion	D. jurisdiction	E. interpreta-tion	18.____
19.	A. auxilary	B. boundaries	C. session	D. fabric	E. ceiling	19.____
20.	A. imperious	B. depreciate	C. rebutal	D. wharf	E. giddy	20.____

KEY (CORRECT ANSWERS)

1.	E.	tendency
2.	A.	committing
3.	B.	surgery
4.	E.	interrupt
5.	D.	mattress
6.	B.	bulletin
7.	D.	sacrifice
8.	E.	fascinate
9.	B.	suspense
10.	C.	repetitious
11.	C.	equipping
12.	C.	management
13.	D.	masterpiece
14.	A.	disappoint
15.	B.	peninsula
16.	C.	primarily
17.	A.	warrior
18.	B.	lubricant
19.	A.	auxiliary
20.	C.	rebuttal

TEST 5

DIRECTIONS: In each question of the following tests, select the letter of the one MISSPELLED word in each of the listed groups of five (5) words. *PRINT THE LETTER OF THE CORRECT ANSWER IN THE SPACE AT THE RIGHT.*

1.	A. renewel	B. charitable	C. abrupt	D. humankind	E. strengthen	1.____
2.	A. khaki	B. survival	C. laboratory	D. intensefied	E. stature	2.____
3.	A. diesel	B. cocoa	C. alphabetti-cal	D. visible	E. overlaid	3.____
4.	A. neutral	B. ballot	C. parallysis	D. enterprise	E. abnormal	4.____
5.	A. ironical	B. mountain-ous	C. permissible	D. carburetor	E. blizard	5.____
6.	A. penalty	B. affidavit	C. document	D. notery	E. valid	6.____
7.	A. provocative	B. apparition	C. forfiet	D. procedure	E. requisite	7.____
8.	A. terrifying	B. museum	C. minimum	D. competitors	E. efficiensy	8.____
9.	A. hangar	B. spokesman	C. mustache	D. cathederal	E. pumpkin	9.____
10.	A. guidance	B. until	C. usage	D. loyalist	E. prarie	10.____
11.	A. obnoxious	B. balancing	C. squadron	D. illicit	E. clearence	11.____
12.	A. timetable	B. gymnasium	C. humid	D. disolve	E. gracious	12.____
13.	A. spiciness	B. biblography	C. injunction	D. mediator	E. discrimi-nate	13.____
14.	A. endearing	B. mannerism	C. predeces-ser	D. gardener	E. instanta-neous	14.____
15.	A. shrewd-ness	B. purified	C. acceptable	D. uniqueness	E. corugated	15.____
16.	A. baptize	B. diversity	C. parochial	D. abandon-ning	E. hypnosis	16.____
17.	A. deteryorate	B. priority	C. cuddle	D. shrivel	E. narcotic	17.____
18.	A. neutrality	B. horserad-ish	C. contemporar-ies	D. inducement	E. prelimnery	18.____
19.	A. eventually	B. disilu-sioned	C. divine	D. inimitable	E. fraudulent	19.____
20.	A. verticle	B. musician	C. tomatoes	D. athletic	E. decision	20.____

KEY (CORRECT ANSWERS)

1. A. renewal
2. D. intensified
3. C. alphabetical
4. C. paralysis
5. E. blizzard
6. D. notary
7. C. forfeit
8. E. efficiency
9. D. cathedral
10. E. prairie
11. E. clearance
12. D. dissolve
13. B. bibliography
14. C. predecessor
15. E. corrugated
16. D. abandoning
17. A. deteriorate
18. E. preliminary
19. B. disillusioned
20. A. vertical

TEST 6

DIRECTIONS: In each question of the following tests, select the letter of the one MISSPELLED word in each of the listed groups of five (5) words. *PRINT THE LETTER OF THE CORRECT ANSWER IN THE SPACE AT THE RIGHT.*

1.	A. advising	B. recognize	C. seize	D. supply	E. tradegy	1.____
2.	A. intensive	B. stationary	C. benifit	D. equipped	E. preferring	2.____
3.	A. predjudice	B. pervade	C. excel	D. capitol	E. chimneys	3.____
4.	A. all right	B. ninty	C. cronies	D. nervous	E. separate	4.____
5.	A. atheletic	B. queue	C. furl	D. schedule	E. abusing	5.____
6.	A. skein	B. wholesome	C. witches	D. coherent	E. defenite	6.____
7.	A. aggravate	B. counsel	C. deplorable	D. proficency	E. catarrh	7.____
8.	A. suppressed	B. lugubrious	C. pecuniary	D. boulevard	E. fourty-fourth	8.____
9.	A. militarism	B. pilot	C. crimnal	D. monoto-nous	E. tendency	9.____
10.	A. prevalent	B. berth	C. auxiliary	D. priveleges	E. women's	10.____
11.	A. incurred	B. cieling	C. strengthen	D. carnage	E. typical	11.____
12.	A. twins	B. year's	C. acutely	D. changible	E. facility	12.____
13.	A. deliscious	B. enormous	C. likeness	D. witnesses	E. commodity	13.____
14.	A. scenes	B. enlarge-ment	C. discretion	D. acknowledg-ing	E. sesion	14.____
15.	A. annum	B. strenuous	C. tretchery	D. infamy	E. opportune	15.____
16.	A. marmelade	B. loot	C. kinsman	D. crochet	E. hawser	16.____
17.	A. fireman	B. glossary	C. tuition	D. dissapoint	E. refrigerator	17.____
18.	A. inadequate	B. municpal	C. bored	D. masonic	E. utilize	18.____
19.	A. partisan	B. temporary	C. cawle-flower	D. obstinacy	E. hyperbole	19.____
20.	A. people's	B. spherical	C. foliage	D. everlasting	E. feesable	20.____

KEY (CORRECT ANSWERS)

1. E. tragedy
2. C. benefit
3. A. prejudice
4. B. ninety
5. A. athletic
6. E. definite
7. D. proficiency
8. E. forty-fourth
9. C. criminal
10. D. privileges
11. B. ceiling
12. D. changeable
13. A. delicious
14. E. session
15. C. treachery
16. A. marmalade
17. D. disappoint
18. B. municipal
19. C. cauliflower
20. E. feasible

TEST 7

DIRECTIONS: In each question of the following tests, select the letter of the one MIS-SPELLED word in each of the listed groups of five (5) words. *PRINT THE LETTER OF THE CORRECT ANSWER IN THE SPACE AT THE RIGHT.*

1.	A. inferred	B. whisle	C. jovial	D. conscript	E. gracious	1.____
2.	A. tantalizing	B. ominous	C. conductor	D. duchess	E. telagram	2.____
3.	A. reconcile	B. primitive	C. sausy	D. quinine	E. cede	3.____
4.	A. immagine	B. viaduct	C. chisel	D. Saturn	E. currant	4.____
5.	A. amplify	B. greace	C. cholera	D. perilous	E. theology	5.____
6.	A. pursevere	B. deodorize	C. ligament	D. illuminate	E. dropsy	6.____
7.	A. legible	B. frivolously	C. precious	D. rezem-blence	E. congeal	7.____
8.	A. intramural	B. epidemic	C. germicide	D. anonymous	E. acurracy	8.____
9.	A. affable	B. hazard	C. combust-able	D. lacquer	E. stationary	9.____
10.	A. sagacious	B. interpreter	C. poultise	D. dinosaur	E. dismal	10.____
11.	A. acknowledg-ing	B. deligate	C. foliage	D. staid	E. loot	11.____
12.	A. gardian	B. losing	C. notwithstand-ing	D. worlds	E. typhoid	12.____
13.	A. medal	B. utilize	C. efficiency	D. apricot	E. soliceting	13.____
14.	A. museum	B. Christian	C. possesion	D. occasional	E. bored	14.____
15.	A. capitol	B. sieze	C. premises	D. fragrance	E. tonnage	15.____
16.	A. requisition	B. faculties	C. canon	D. chaufur	E. stomach	16.____
17.	A. solemn	B. ascertain	C. I'll	D. chef	E. delinquant	17.____
18.	A. parliments	B. distributor	C. voluntary	D. lovable	E. counsel	18.____
19.	A. morale	B. democrat	C. rhumatism	D. dormitory	E. leased	19.____
20.	A. screech	B. missapropriat-ing	C. courtesies	D. wretched	E. furlough	20.____

KEY (CORRECT ANSWERS)

1.	B.	whistle
2.	E.	telegram
3.	C.	saucy
4.	A.	imagine
5.	B.	grease
6.	A.	persevere
7.	D.	resemblance
8.	E.	accuracy
9.	C.	combustible
10.	C.	poultice
11.	B.	delegate
12.	A.	guardian
13.	E.	soliciting
14.	C.	possession
15.	B.	seize
16.	D.	chauffeur
17.	E.	delinquent
18.	A.	parliaments
19.	C.	rheumatism
20.	B.	misappropriating

TEST 8

DIRECTIONS: In each question of the following tests, select the letter of the one MISSPELLED word in each of the listed groups of five (5) words. *PRINT THE LETTER OF THE CORRECT ANSWER IN THE SPACE AT THE RIGHT.*

1.	A. typhoid	B. tarriff	C. visible	D. accent	E. countries	1.____
2.	A. dizzy	B. leggings	C. steak	D. compaine	E. interior	2.____
3.	A. profit	B. tiranny	C. shocked	D. response	E. innocent	3.____
4.	A. freshman	B. vague	C. larsiny	D. ignorant	E. worrying	4.____
5.	A. disatesfied	B. jealous	C. unfortunately	D. economical	E. lettuce	5.____
6.	A. based	B. primarily	C. condemned	D. accompanied	E. dupped	6.____
7.	A. superntendant	B. veil	C. congenial	D. quantities	E. ere	7.____
8.	A. unanimous	B. dessert	C. undoubtedly	D. kolera	E. nuisance	8.____
9.	A. woman's	B. bulletin	C. 'tis	D. Pullman	E. envellop	9.____
10.	A. initiate	B. guardian	C. pagent	D. wretched	E. adieu	10.____
11.	A. continually	B. guild	C. vegtable	D. vague	E. patience	11.____
12.	A. desease	B. parole	C. gallery	D. awkward	E. you'd	12.____
13.	A. border	B. warrant	C. operated	D. economics	E. ilegal	13.____
14.	A. fatal	B. agatation	C. obliged	D. studying	E. resignation	14.____
15.	A. ammendment	B. promptness	C. glimpse	D. canon	E. tract	15.____
16.	A. wholly	B. apricot	C. destruction	D. pappal	E. leisure	16.____
17.	A. issuing	B. rabbid	C. unauthorized	D. parasite	E. khaki	17.____
18.	A. nowadays	B. courtesies	C. negotiate	D. gaurdian	E. derrick	18.____
19.	A. partisan	B. seanse	C. vacancy	D. fragrance	E. corps	19.____
20.	A. equipped	B. nuisance	C. phrenoligist	D. foreign	E. insignia	20.____

KEY (CORRECT ANSWERS)

1. B. tariff
2. D. company
3. B. tyranny
4. C. larceny
5. A. dissatisfied
6. E. duped
7. A. superintendent
8. D. cholera
9. E. envelope
10. C. pageant
11. C. vegetable
12. A. disease
13. E. illegal
14. B. agitation
15. A. amendment
16. D. papal
17. B. rabid
18. D. guardian
19. B. seance
20. C. phrenologist

TEST 9

DIRECTIONS: In each question of the following tests, select the letter of the one MISSPELLED word in each of the listed groups of five (5) words. *PRINT THE LETTER OF THE CORRECT ANSWER IN THE SPACE AT THE RIGHT*

1.	A. frightfully	B. mantain	C. post office	D. specific	E. bachelor	1.____
2.	A. cease	B. turkeys	C. woman's	D. hustling	E. weild	2.____
3.	A. expedition	B. valuoble	C. typhoid	D. grapevines	E. advice	3.____
4.	A. echoes	B. absolutly	C. foggy	D. wretched	E. Sabbath	4.____
5.	A. screech	B. motorist	C. congre-sionel	D. utilize	E. eligible	5.____
6.	A. quizzes	B. coarse	C. aquain-tence	D. exhibition	E. totally	6.____
7.	A. principle	B. transferring	C. statutes	D. here's	E. sergeon	7.____
8.	A. porcilane	B. primeval	C. suite	D. unautho-rized	E. declension	8.____
9.	A. commodity	B. mischevi-ous	C. galvanized	D. ordinance	E. tuition	9.____
10.	A. Christian	B. fraternity	C. accompany-ing	D. disernable	E. inadequate	10.____
11.	A. subsidy	B. inference	C. chronicle	D. purchace	E. adroit	11.____
12.	A. resources	B. cargoes	C. oponent	D. disbelief	E. treasurer	12.____
13.	A. origional	B. provincial	C. knuckle	D. ridiculous	E. ecstasy	13.____
14.	A. attitude	B. soloes	C. occurred	D. policies	E. technique	14.____
15.	A. opinionated	B. quantity	C. systematic	D. drought	E. confiden-cial	15.____
16.	A. interim	B. idleness	C. accesion	D. elite	E. fungi	16.____
17.	A. inarticulate	B. servitude	C. ejaculate	D. herewith	E. pre-ceedence	17.____
18.	A. experimen-tal	B. minority	C. cultural	D. expedient	E. penant	18.____
19.	A. apparently	B. criticism	C. justification	D. physican	E. simulta-neous	19.____
20.	A. acciden-tally	B. overule	C. uninten-tional	D. talented	E. maturation	20.____

KEY (CORRECT ANSWERS)

1. B. maintain
2. E. wield
3. B. valuable
4. B. absolutely
5. C. congressional
6. C. acquaintance
7. E. surgeon
8. A. porcelain
9. B. mischievous
10. D. discernible
11. D. purchase
12. C. opponent
13. A. original
14. B. solos
15. E. confidential
16. C. accession
17. E. precedence
18. E. pennant
19. D. physician
20. B. overrule

TEST 10

DIRECTIONS: In each question of the following tests, select the letter of the one MISSPELLED word in each of the listed groups of five (5) words. *PRINT THE LETTER OF THE CORRECT ANSWER IN THE SPACE AT THE RIGHT.*

1.	A. liabillity	B. capacity	C. guidance	D. illegible	E. expedient	1.____
2.	A. debris	B. apetite	C. mosquitoes	D. vessal	E. yacht	2.____
3.	A. tireless	B. feindish	C. recruit	D. swarthy	E. sandal	3.____
4.	A. redouble	B. wizard	C. murdurer	D. hindrance	E. syncope	4.____
5.	A. equalize	B. turbulent	C. repetitive	D. corronation	E. statistical	5.____
6.	A. remittance	B. sensitivity	C. fatality	D. soprano	E. inconve-niance	6.____
7.	A. fraternity	B. plebeian	C. inteligible	D. trickster	E. expedition-ary	7.____
8.	A. gasous	B. consis-tency	C. brooches	D. magistrate	E. translucent	8.____
9.	A. lightning	B. persistent	C. cynical	D. musician	E. recipricate	9.____
10.	A. commodity	B. fictitous	C. rabid	D. gaiety	E. couldn't	10.____
11.	A. visible	B. creditor	C. paradice	D. infinite	E. question-naire	11.____
12.	A. existence	B. disarming	C. endorse-ment	D. commercal	E. trigger	12.____
13.	A. aluminum	B. stuning	C. allowance	D. irate	E. pleasantry	13.____
14.	A. cipher	B. colloquial	C. envoy	D. pursued	E. writting	14.____
15.	A. insurable	B. benign	C. influentual	D. sophomore	E. casualty	15.____
16.	A. presenti-ment	B. theological	C. anatamy	D. eccentricity	E. amphibious	16.____
17.	A. embargo	B. vocalize	C. recom-mend	D. confering	E. remunerate	17.____
18.	A. tangent	B. fickel	C. circuit	D. mathemat-ics	E. vegetarian	18.____
19.	A. unsched-uled	B. declension	C. secretariat	D. forsight	E. enamel	19.____
20.	A. hygienic	B. arrogant	C. disbanded	D. census	E. memoran-dem	20.____

KEY (CORRECT ANSWERS)

1. A. liability
2. B. appetite
3. B. fiendish
4. C. murderer
5. D. coronation
6. E. inconvenience
7. C. intelligible
8. A. gaseous
9. E. reciprocate
10. B. fictitious
11. C. paradise
12. D. commercial
13. B. stunning
14. E. writing
15. C. influential
16. C. anatomy
17. D. conferring
18. B. fickle
19. D. foresight
20. E. memorandum